REGENTS RESTORATION DRAMA SERIES

General Editor: John Loftis

THE FAIR PENITENT

NICHOLAS ROWE

The Fair Penitent

Edited by

MALCOLM GOLDSTEIN

UNIVERSITY OF NEBRASKA PRESS · LINCOLN

MANUFACTURED IN THE UNITED STATES OF AMERICA

Regents Restoration Drama Series

The Regents Restoration Drama Series provides soundly edited texts, in modern spelling, of the more significant plays of the late seventeenth and early eighteenth centuries. The word "Restoration" is here used ambiguously and must be explained. If to the historian it refers to the period between 1660 and 1685 (or 1688), it has long been used by the student of drama in default of a more precise word to refer to plays belonging to the dramatic tradition established in the 1660's, weakening after 1700, and displaced in the 1730's. It is in this extended sense—imprecise though justified by academic custom—that the word is used in this series, which includes plays first produced between 1660 and 1737. Although these limiting dates are determined by political events, the return of Charles II (and the removal of prohibitions against operation of theaters) and the passage of Walpole's Stage Licensing Act, they enclose a period of dramatic history having a coherence of its own in the establishment, development, and disintegration of a tradition.

Some seventeen editions having appeared as this volume goes to press, the series has reached over a third of its anticipated range of between forty and fifty volumes. The volumes will continue to be published for a number of years, at the rate of three or more annually. From the beginning the editors have planned the series with attention to the projected dimensions of the completed whole, a representative collection of Restoration drama providing a record of artistic achievement and providing also a record of the deepest concerns of three generations of Englishmen. And thus it contains deservedly famous plays—*The Country Wife, The Man of Mode,* and *The Way of the World*—and also significant but little known plays, *The Virtuoso,* for example, and *City Politiques,* the former a satirical review of scientific investigation in the early years of the Royal Society, the latter an equally satirical review of politics at the time of the Popish Plot. If the volumes of famous plays finally achieve the larger circulation, the other volumes may conceivably have the greater utility, in making available texts otherwise difficult of access with the editorial apparatus needed to make them intelligible.

The editors have had the instructive example of the parallel and senior project, the Regents Renaissance Drama Series; they have in fact used the editorial policies developed for the earlier plays as their own, modifying them as appropriate for the later period and as the experience of successive editions suggested. The introductions to the separate Restoration plays differ considerably in their nature. Although a uniform body of relevant information is presented in each of them, no attempt has been made to impose a pattern of interpretation. Emphasis in the introductions has necessarily varied with the nature of the plays and inevitably—we think desirably—with the special interests and aptitudes of the different editors.

Each text in the series is based on a fresh collation of the seventeenth- and eighteenth-century editions that might be presumed to have authority. The textual notes, which appear above the rule at the bottom of each page, record all substantive departures from the edition used as the copy-text. Variant substantive readings among contemporary editions are listed there as well. Editions later than the eighteenth century are referred to in the textual notes only when an emendation originating in some one of them is received into the text. Variants of accidentals (spelling, punctuation, capitalization) are not recorded in the notes. Contracted forms of characters' names are silently expanded in speech prefixes and stage directions and, in the case of speech prefixes, are regularized. Additions to the stage directions of the copy-text are enclosed in brackets.

Spelling has been modernized along consciously conservative lines, but within the limits of a modernized text the linguistic quality of the original has been carefully preserved. Contracted preterites have regularly been expanded. Punctuation has been brought into accord with modern practices. The objective has been to achieve a balance between the pointing of the old editions and a system of punctuation which, without overloading the text with exclamation marks, semicolons, and dashes, will make the often loosely flowing verse and prose of the original syntactically intelligible to the modern reader. Dashes are regularly used only to indicate interrupted speeches, or shifts of address within a single speech.

Explanatory notes, chiefly concerned with glossing obsolete words and phrases, are printed below the textual notes at the bottom of each page. References to stage directions in the notes follow the admirable system of the Revels editions, whereby stage directions are keyed, decimally, to the line of the text before or after which they occur. Thus, a note on 0.2 has reference to the second line of the stage direction at the beginning of the scene in question. A note on 115.1 has reference to the first line of the stage direction following line 115 of the text of the relevant scene. Speech prefixes, and any stage directions attached to them, are keyed to the first line of accompanying dialogue.

JOHN LOFTIS

April, 1968
Stanford University

Contents

List of Abbreviations

Q   Quarto, 1703

D1   First Duodecimo (duplicate issues), 1714

D2   Second Duodecimo, 1714

D3   Third Duodecimo, 1718

JRS   J. R. Sutherland, ed. *Three Plays by Nicholas Rowe*. London, 1929.

MJ   Dougald MacMillan and Howard Mumford Jones, eds. *Plays of the Restoration and Eighteenth Century*. New York, 1931.

S.D.   stage direction

Introduction

In the *Post Boy* for March 4–6 and 9–11, 1703, advertisements announced the publication of a prologue to *The Fair Penitent*, designed to be spoken by Thomas Betterton but "refused." No author's name is given, and the identity of the publisher is concealed behind the phrase "Printed for the Booksellers of London and Westminster." Jacob Tonson advertised the publication of the play itself in the *Post Boy* for March 13–16, "As it is Acted at the New Theatre in Little Lincolns-Inn-Fields." The date of the first performance is not on record, but the evidence of these three notices places it within the first two weeks of March.

The first edition was published in quarto: a copy at the University of Texas provides the copy-text for the present edition in modern spelling. This copy, like others I have seen at the Folger Shakespeare Library (three copies), Yale, and Columbia, is printed with advertisements for books published by Tonson. The Henry E. Huntington Library and the New York Public Library have copies that are printed without the advertisements but do not reveal substantive variants. They do not appear to represent a separate issue. The quarto was followed in Rowe's lifetime by three editions in duodecimo. The first was published in 1714 and was reissued once during the year. One issue is designated the second edition on the title page, but the other lacks this designation; otherwise they are identical. I have not been able to discover the order in which they were published. The second duodecimo, also dated 1714, follows the pagination of the first and has the same ornaments, but is completely reset. Although it is not so designated on the title page and has not previously been identified as such, it is the third edition of the play. It includes all the substantive alterations of the 1703 text that appear in the first duodecimo, along with others that appear in the third. I have examined copies at Columbia and the Folger. Although the third duodecimo, published in 1718, is designated the third edition on the title page, it is in fact the fourth. It follows the pagination of the earlier duodecimos, but is a new setting. The British Museum's

General Catalogue of Printed Books lists an octavo edition of 1703, but the copy referred to lacks a title page and bears no indication of its date. On examination, it proves to be identical with an octavo in the Folger that is catalogued as having been printed by Thomas Johnson at The Hague, *ca.* 1721.

Although it is no longer acted, *The Fair Penitent* was one of the most successful plays of the eighteenth century. Emmett L. Avery has found that, exclusive of Shakespeare's works, it was the sixth most frequently performed tragedy in the London theaters between 1702 and 1776.[1] For the first twelve years following its opening no performances are on record, but from 1715 until the end of the century it was presented in almost every theatrical season, and it is known to have been presented several times in the nineteenth century. In the original production the most distinguished actors of Lincoln's Inn Fields appeared in the leading parts: Thomas Betterton as Horatio, John Verbruggen as Altamont, George Powell as Lothario, Elizabeth Barry as Calista, and Anne Bracegirdle as Lavinia. Among the great players who took roles in later productions were James Quin (Horatio), Barton Booth (Lothario), Anne Oldfield (Calista), Susannah Cibber (Lucilla and Calista), George Anne Bellamy (Lavinia and Calista), David Garrick (Lothario and Sciolto), Charles Macklin (Sciolto), Spranger Barry (Horatio, Lothario, and Sciolto), Peg Woffington (Calista and Lothario), Mary Ann Yates (Calista), Elizabeth Younge (Calista), Sarah Siddons (Calista), John Philip Kemble (Horatio and Sciolto), and Charles Kemble (Lothario) —in the order of their first appearances in the play.[2] It is not difficult to imagine the excitement created by performances in which such actors gave life to the scenes.

The Fair Penitent is an unacknowledged adaptation of Philip Massinger and Nathan Field's *The Fatal Dowry*, a play published in 1632 but probably written between 1616 and 1619.[3] Although Rowe's

[1] Emmett L. Avery, "The Popularity of *The Mourning Bride* in the London Theaters in the Eighteenth Century," *Research Studies of the State College of Washington*, IX (1941), 115–116.

[2] For 1703–1776 see *The London Stage 1660–1800*, Parts 2–4, ed. Emmett L. Avery, Arthur H. Scouten, and George Winchester Stone, Jr. (Carbondale, Ill., 1960–1962); for 1777–1830 see John Genest, *Some Account of the English Stage from the Restoration in 1660 to 1830* (Bath, 1832), V–IX.

[3] Gerald Eades Bentley, *The Jacobean and Caroline Stage*, IV (Oxford, 1956), 783–784.

failure to acknowledge a specific source carries the suggestion that he wished his play to be taken as original, it seems likely enough that he expected the source to be recognized. The habit of borrowing old plots was as common with Augustan playwrights as it had been with the playwrights of the Renaissance, and audiences on the whole were tolerant of the practice. Strongly worded complaints such as those of Gerard Langbaine in *Momus Triumphans* (1687) and *An Account of the English Dramatic Poets* (1691) had not put an end to it, and, for that matter, neither did the acid expressions of disapproval that Alexander Pope later inserted into *The Dunciad*.[4] The only contemporary critic to mention Rowe's source, so far as is known, was Charles Gildon, who referred to it in *A New Rehearsal* (1714), a prolonged attack on Rowe's dramatic writing. But even this hostile critic refrained from calling Rowe a plagiarist and was content to stop with the assertion that *The Fatal Dowry* is the better of the two tragedies.[5] In the old play Rowe found a good plot, if a simple one, to which he gave an attractive, modern ring.[6]

Of Rowe's revisions of the material supplied by Massinger and Field, most are indicative of the taste of the age for regularity and decorum. They illustrate the differences between the panoramic drama of the English Renaissance, with its origin in the wide-ranging mystery cycles of the Middle Ages, and the "unified," tightly constructed drama preferred by Augustan writers and audiences. At the same time, they reveal the special characteristics of Rowe's own taste and talent.

The effort to impose the unities of time, place, and action on the plot of *The Fatal Dowry* is evident at virtually every moment. In Massinger and Field, the first act, which includes a long courtroom scene, establishes the courage and dignity of Charalois (Altamont in *The Fair Penitent*), informs the audience of the ill treatment accorded

---

[4] Among the many dramatists of the early eighteenth century in addition to Rowe who borrowed plots are Susannah Centlivre, Colley Cibber, Sir Richard Steele, and Sir John Vanbrugh, to name only four of the most successful.

[5] Charles Gildon, *A New Rehearsal* (London, 1714), pp. 57–58.

[6] Aaron Hill's *The Insolvent: or, Filial Piety*, produced posthumously (and unsuccessfully) in 1758, should be mentioned as another adaptation of *The Fatal Dowry*—but at one remove, since it is said to be based on a manuscript play titled *The Guiltless Adultress*, attributed to Sir William D'Avenant. Hill's play is tragic in tone, but ends happily. On the history of its composition see Hill, *Dramatic Works* (London, 1760), II, [331]–333.

his father, and shows Rochfort (Rowe's Sciolto) moved to pity for
Charalois in his distress. In Rowe's play these events have occurred
in the past and are presented through expository dialogue between
Altamont and Horatio. Similarly, an expository scene informs the
audience of Lothario's seduction of Calista; this has taken place well
in the past, not, as in *The Fatal Dowry*, in the course of the play and
after the wedding ceremony. The neoclassical instinct for compression
led also to a reduction in the cast of characters. Whereas Massinger
and Field provide fifteen parts identified by name and a regiment of
smaller, unnamed supporting roles, Rowe employs only eight characters bearing names, along with a few servants of Sciolto. The re-
naming of characters is typical of adaptations, and so is the change of
locale. The removal of the action from Dijon to Genoa is not meaning-
ful, for Genoa to Rowe is merely another foreign city whose inhabi-
tants, not being English, are exotic and can perform acts that would
be beyond credibility if performed by Englishmen. The city is no
more Italian than French. It exists only in the vaguely described,
remote land of most English neoclassical tragedy—a fantasy land
even when given a recognizable name. Holding to Augustan principles
of dramatic construction, Rowe forces so vast an action into one day
of life in a palace and its environs that the unities of time and place
produce an effect of timelessness and placelessness.[7]

Rowe's most interesting departure from his source, and the one
most significant to his theme, is his shift of focus from the bridegroom
to the bride. Calista is his tragic protagonist. *The Fair Penitent* is the
first of Rowe's three "she-tragedies," preceding by a decade *The
Tragedy of Jane Shore* (1714) and *The Tragedy of Lady Jane Gray* (1715).
Rowe himself is the presumed inventor of the term, its first recorded
use occurring in his epilogue to *Jane Shore*.

The roles of all three heroines are stageworthy, and for them
Rowe deserves, and has received, praise. He is not, however, the first
dramatist, not even the first dramatist of his own time, to write ample
feminine roles. The modern use of the term "she-tragedy" in connec-
tion with Rowe obscures the fact that plays with tragic heroines
have appeared since antiquity; Clytemnestra, Antigone, and Hecuba
are after all among the most forceful personalities in dramatic

[7] For detailed comparisons of the two plays see W. Gifford, ed., *The Plays
of Philip Massinger* (London, 1805), III, 453–472; and Donald B. Cook,
"An Eighteenth-Century Adaptation of Massinger," *Modern Language
Quarterly*, XIII (1952), 239–252.

literature. Impressive heroines are present in the tragedies of the English Renaissance in greater numbers than they may seem to be. If Shakespeare's Cleopatra is the most womanly of all, his Juliet and Lady Macbeth are no less memorable, and countless actresses have found them to be grateful parts. The number of large-scale roles for women written between 1660 and 1700, when playwrights knew that they would in fact be played by women, is of course very great. It would be an error not to recognize the opportunities for attention and applause awaiting the actresses who took such parts as Statira and Roxana in Nathaniel Lee's *The Rival Queens* and Monimia in Thomas Otway's *The Orphan*, to say nothing of John Dryden's many unhappy heroines and those of John Banks.[8] The feminine roles in these plays are the more prominent because of the tendency of neoclassical authors to tighten their action and to include only such characters as seem essential to the unraveling of a plot.

That able actresses should be available to playwrights in a country that before 1660 had no tradition of women in the theater is not so strange as we may be inclined to think. Passable acting talent is common enough everywhere, however rare genius may be; no doubt many young women of Shakespeare's time played Juliet capably to their mirrors. In any event, Rowe was fortunate indeed in the casting of his play, for Mrs. Barry and Mrs. Bracegirdle were two of the most accomplished actresses of the age; it is likely that he wrote with them in mind and designed their roles to display their particular skills, for they had appeared in his first two plays. In 1703 both were nearing the end of brilliant careers, during which they frequently acted together.[9]

Rowe's exploration of the thoughts and feelings of his characters, and especially those of Calista, is more probing than was possible for Massinger and Field in their panoramic play with many minor roles and with prolonged scenes recounting affairs of state. The character of Calista is not only more substantial, but softer, more vulnerable, and more appealing than that of Beaumelle, her counterpart in *The Fatal Dowry*. It has long been argued that she does not regret her sin

---

[8] On this writer see Thomas Marshall Howe Blair, ed., John Banks, *The Unhappy Favourite; or The Earl of Essex* (New York, 1939), pp. [3]–29.

[9] On the type-casting of these actresses see Eric Rothstein, *Restoration Tragedy; Form and the Process of Change* (Madison, 1967), pp. 141–144; for biographical sketches see John Harold Wilson, *All the King's Ladies: Actresses of the Restoration* (Chicago, 1958), pp. 110–117, 122–127.

of the flesh so much as its having been found out. Theophilus Cibber, for example, believed that "the Fair Wanton" would be a more accurate phrase for her than the epithet chosen by Rowe.[10] Samuel Johnson's remark about her may recall Cibber's: "It has been observed that the title of the play does not sufficiently correspond with the behavior of Calista, who at last shews no evident signs of repentance, but may be reasonably suspected of feeling pain from detection rather than from guilt, and expresses more shame than sorrow, and more rage than shame."[11] Like John Downes before him, Johnson preferred the early scenes of the play to the catastrophe; the fifth act he regarded as chiefly a discussion of past events.[12] Yet it is in the fifth act that Calista makes her most vivid appearance. Modern readers, familiar with the effort of mid-twentieth-century dramatists to analyze the minds of greatly distressed characters, may find Calista's last, harrowing scenes the most engrossing of the tragedy. Alone in the charnel house as the fifth act begins, she listens to a bleak, melancholy song and gazes at the bier of the "gay Lothario," as she then calls her lover. Tossing aside a book of instruction in penitence—not a Bible, it should be noted—she grieves over the corpse. A modern critic has observed of this scene that Calista is not rejecting penitence as such, but only the notion that it can be achieved through art—that is, by means of a book.[13] Suicide is her only escape. It is required by the demands of poetic justice, to be sure, yet is also a practical step, for in no other way can she put an end to self-loathing.

If Calista lacks grandeur, if her fall does not cause the heavens to weep, it is by Rowe's firm intention. The play is deliberately held within the range of the family circle. It is a domestic tragedy whose heroine is not a woman of command, but a distraught mistress and wife. In the prologue Rowe deplores the proliferation of tragedies about highly placed persons and describes his work as a "melancholy tale of private woes"; it is, in other words, a story of such troubles as ordinary persons encounter in the progress of their lives. The character of Calista provides a compelling portrait of humanity troubled by

[10] Theophilus Cibber, *The Lives of the Poets of Great Britain and Ireland* (London, 1753), III, 276.

[11] Samuel Johnson, *Lives of the English Poets*, ed. George Birkbeck Hill (Oxford, 1905), II, 68.

[12] John Downes, *Roscius Anglicanus; or, an Historical Review of the Stage from 1660 to 1706* (London, 1708), p. 46; Johnson, *loc. cit.*

[13] Lindley A. Wyman, "The Tradition of the Formal Meditation in Rowe's *The Fair Penitent*," *Philological Quarterly*, XLII (1963), 416.

conflicting passions. She is ashamed of having yielded to Lothario, but she loves him nevertheless and resents the double standard of sexual behavior. Nowhere is the strength of her feeling more evident than in her ringing speech against that standard:

> How hard is the condition of our sex,
> Through ev'ry state of life the slaves of man!
> In all the dear, delightful days of youth
> A rigid father dictates to our wills,
> And deals out pleasure with a scanty hand;
> To his, the tyrant husband's reign succeeds;
> Proud with opinion of superior reason,
> He holds domestic business and devotion
> All we are capable to know, and shuts us,
> Like cloistered idiots, from the world's acquaintance
> And all the joys of freedom; wherefore are we
> Born with high souls but to assert ourselves,
> Shake off this vile obedience they exact,
> And claim an equal empire o'er the world?
>
> (III. 39–52)

Yet in the end this intelligent woman finds it impossible to live without honor.

Of the leading male characters, Lothario, the archetypal young romancer, is the most prominent, even though Sciolto, Horatio, and Altamont have longer roles. Sciolto, the stoic father; Horatio, the faithful friend; Altamont, the deceived bridegroom—all are familiar stage presences. Like most sympathetic characters in neoclassical tragedy, the three are caught in conflicts between love and honor. Altamont, who has the central masculine role, is surprisingly deficient in vigor. Lucilla, Calista's confidante, speaks of him as "Kind as the softest virgin of our sex"; and even if the words are intended as a compliment, they reflect the weakness of his personality. As Calista grows in the course of the play, he seems to fade. Not only is he less virile than the other male characters; he is no match for his headstrong wife. Theophilus Cibber noted that the role was difficult to act, and Francis Gentleman described it as insipid.[14]

Rowe offered a stronger role in the character of Lothario. Johnson was the first of many critics to see the outline of Lothario's personality

[14] Cibber, III, 277; Francis Gentleman, *The Dramatic Censor; or, Critical Companion* (London, 1770), I, 273.

in the character of Lovelace, the unprincipled rake of Samuel
Richardson's *Clarissa* (1747–1748). In his view, Richardson's work
was an improvement upon Rowe, for "Lothario, with gaiety which
cannot be hated, and bravery which cannot be despised, retains too
much of the spectator's kindness."[15] Certainly Lothario is a more
attractive character than Lovelace, for he is no rapist, and he declares
in the first act that he would have married Calista had not his suit
been rejected by Sciolto.[16] But if he is more attractive than the morally
superior Altamont, this is not a weakness in the play, for it is his
attractiveness that creates the turmoil in the heart and mind of
Calista, in which the force of the tragedy consists.

The language of the play is its greatest weakness. Passages of
pathetic diction too soft for the events they describe appear in each of
the acts. Rowe attempted in *Jane Shore* to imitate the style of Shakespeare and went so far as to proclaim on the title page that he had
done so. But the most obvious stylistic influence on *The Fair Penitent*
is the work of Otway, a playwright nearer to his own time. In
particular, *The Orphan* abounds with melting phrases of the sort that
Rowe gave to his sympathetic characters, no doubt with the intention
of enhancing the domestic quality of the action. The speeches of
Lavinia make calculated assaults on the feelings of the audience. At
moments of anxiety she resorts to images of smallness—"little heart,"
"little wealth"—as though to take on the appeal of a child. In the
first act this naive woman experiences a shock on hearing from her
husband that not all partners in marriage are faithful to their spouses:

> Can there be such? And have they peace of mind?
> Have they in all the series of their changing
> One happy hour? If women are such things,
> How was I formed so different from my sex?
> My little heart is satisfied with you;
> You take up all her room . . . .
>   (I. 392–397)

In the third act, after collapsing from her unsuccessful effort to mend
the broken friendship of her brother and her husband, she rises to
exclaim:

---

[15] Johnson, II, 67.

[16] See H. G. Ward, "Richardson's Character of Lovelace," *Modern
Language Review*, VII (1912), [494]–498.

INTRODUCTION

Is there not cause for weeping? O, Horatio!
A brother and a husband were my treasure;
'Twas all the little wealth that poor Lavinia
Saved from the shipwreck of her father's fortunes.
One half is lost already; if thou leav'st me,
If thou shouldst prove unkind to me as Altamont,
Whom shall I find to pity my distress,
To have compassion on a helpless wanderer,
And give her where to lay her wretched head?
                                    (III, 361–369)

Calista's language also is adorned with affective images, but it is
generally more vigorous, as in the passage on the station of women
quoted above. When Rowe falters in shaping her speeches, he some-
times provokes a smile. Bonamy Dobrée has pointed out a line spoken
by Calista in the fourth act that strikes him as unintentionally comic:
"Is it the voice of thunder, or my father?"[17] Another humorous
lapse into ultra-formal diction occurs when, a second before her
death, she addresses Altamont as "thou excellent young man."
Such—and all too familiar—is the primness of the belated convert to
moral rectitude.

I wish to acknowledge that in preparing this edition of *The Fair
Penitent* I frequently and unhesitatingly consulted two earlier editions:
that of J. R. Sutherland and that of Dougald MacMillan and Howard
Mumford Jones. I did not always agree with my predecessors, but
without question my labor was very much lighter with the aid of their
scholarship than it would otherwise have been. I am indebted also
to Professor Lillian Feder, who patiently answered my questions
about Rowe's classical allusions, to Professor William W. Appleton,
who described the misdated octavo edition in the British Museum
to me before I had an opportunity to examine it myself, and to
Professor Shirley Strum Kenny, who gave me invaluable assistance
in dealing with the bibliographical problems of the duodecimo
editions.

                                    Malcolm Goldstein
Queens College of the City University of New York

[17] Bonamy Dobrée, *Restoration Tragedy 1660–1720* (Oxford, 1929), p.156.

THE FAIR PENITENT

Quin morere, ut merita es, ferroque averte dolorem.
Virg. Æn. Lib. 4.

Quin . . . dolorem.] Why not die as you deserve, and end your pain with a
sword? Virgil, *Aeneid*, IV, l. 547.

To Her Grace the Duchess of Ormonde

MADAM,

   The privilege of poetry (or it may be the vanity of the
pretenders to it) has given 'em a kind of right to pretend, at
the same time, to the favor of those whom their high birth
and excellent qualities have placed in a very distinguishing   5
manner above the rest of the world. If this be not a received
maxim, yet I am sure I am to wish it were, that I may have
at least some kind of excuse for laying this tragedy at your
Grace's feet. I have too much reason to fear that it may
prove but an indifferent entertainment to your Grace, since   10
if I have any way succeeded in it, it has been in describing
those violent passions which have been always strangers to
so happy a temper and so noble and so exalted a virtue as
your Grace is mistress of. Yet for all this I cannot but confess
the vanity which I have, to hope that there may be some-   15
thing so moving in the misfortunes and distress of the play as
may be not altogether unworthy of your Grace's pity. This is
one of the main designs of tragedy, and to excite this
generous pity in the greatest minds may pass for some kind
of success in this way of writing. I am sensible of the pre-   20
sumption I am guilty of by this hope, and how much it is
that I pretend to in your Grace's approbation; if it be my
good fortune to meet with any little share of it, I shall always
look upon it as much more to me than the general applause
of the theater, or even the praise of a good critic. Your   25
Grace's name is the best protection this play can hope for,
since the world, ill-natured as it is, agrees in an universal
respect and deference for your Grace's person and character.
In so censorious an age as this is, where malice furnishes
out all the public conversations, where everybody pulls and   30
is pulled to pieces of course, and where there is hardly such
a thing as being merry but at another's expense, yet by a
public and uncommon justice to the Duchess of Ormonde,
her name has never been mentioned but as it ought, though

Duchess of Ormonde] The Duchess of Ormonde was Mary, daughter of
Henry Somerset, first Duke of Beaufort. She was the second wife of James
Butler, second Duke of Ormonde. The Duke was appointed lord-lieutenant
of Ireland in 1703, a position in which he served until 1707 and again from
1710 to 1712. After the death of Queen Anne he became a Jacobite.

she has beauty enough to provoke detraction from the 35
fairest of her own sex, and virtue enough to make the loose
and dissolute of the other (a very formidable party) her
enemies. Instead of this, they agree to say nothing of her
but what she deserves: that her spirit is worthy of her birth;
her sweetness, of the love and respect of all the world; her 40
piety, of her religion; her service, of her royal mistress; and
her beauty and truth, of her lord; that in short every part
of her character is just, and that she is the best reward for
one of the greatest heroes this age has produced. This,
madam, is what you must allow people everywhere to say; 45
those whom you shall leave behind you in England will
have something further to add: the loss we shall suffer by
your Grace's journey to Ireland; the Queen's pleasure and
the impatient wishes of that nation are about to deprive us
of two of our public ornaments. But there is no arguing 50
against reasons so prevalent as these. Those who shall
lament your Grace's absence will yet acquiesce in the wisdom and justice of Her Majesty's choice, among all whose
royal favors none could be so agreeable, upon a thousand
accounts, to that people as the Duke of Ormonde. With what 55
joy, what acclamations shall they meet a Governor who,
beside their former obligations to his family, has so lately
ventured his life and fortune for their preservation? What
duty, what submission shall they not pay to that authority
which the Queen has delegated to a person so dear to 'em? 60
And with what honor, what respect shall they receive
your Grace, when they look upon you as the noblest and
best pattern Her Majesty could send 'em of her own royal
goodness and personal virtues? They shall behold your
Grace with the same pleasure the English shall take when- 65
ever it shall be their good fortune to see you return to your
native country. In England your Grace is become a public
concern, and as your going away will be attended with a
general sorrow, so your return shall give as general a joy;
and to none of those many, more than to, 70

              Madam,

                Your Grace's
                   most obedient, and
                   most humble servant,
                      N. ROWE 75

PROLOGUE

Spoken by Mr. Betterton

Long has the fate of kings and empires been
The common business of the tragic scene,
As if misfortune made the throne her seat,
And none could be unhappy but the great.
Dearly, 'tis true, each buys the crown he wears,   5
And many are the mighty monarch's cares;
By foreign foes and home-bred factions pressed,
Few are the joys he knows, and short his hours of rest.
Stories like these with wonder we may hear,⎤
But far remote, and in a higher sphere,   ⎬   10
We ne'er can pity what we ne'er can share:⎦
Like distant battles of the Pole and Swede,⎤
Which frugal citizens o'er coffee read,   ⎬
Careless for who shall fail or who succeed.⎦
Therefore an humbler theme our author chose,   15
A melancholy tale of private woes;
No princes here lost royalty bemoan,
But you shall meet with sorrows like your own;
Here see imperious love his vassals treat
As hardly as ambition does the great;   20
See how succeeding passions rage by turns,   ⎤
How fierce the youth with joy and rapture burns,⎬
And how to death, for beauty lost, he mourns.   ⎦

Let no nice taste the poet's art arraign,
If some frail, vicious characters he feign;   25
Who writes should still let nature be his care,   ⎤
Mix shades with lights, and not paint all things fair,⎬
But show you men and women as they are.   ⎦
With deference to the fair he bade me say,
Few to perfection ever found the way;   30

---

12. *Pole and Swede*] Charles XII of Sweden invaded Poland in 1701,
and in the following year he took Warsaw.
    13. *frugal*] At coffeehouses patrons could read the newspapers without
having to buy them.

Many in many parts are known t'excel,
But 'twere too hard for one to act all well;
Whom justly life should through each scene commend,
The maid, the wife, the mistress, and the friend,
This age, 'tis true, has one great instance seen, 35
And heav'n in justice made that one a Queen.

DRAMATIS PERSONAE

Men

SCIOLTO, a nobleman of Genoa, father to Calista	*Mr. Bowman*
ALTAMONT, a young lord, in love with Calista, and designed her husband by Sciolto	*Mr. Verbruggen*
HORATIO, his friend	*Mr. Betterton*
LOTHARIO, a young lord, enemy to Altamont	*Mr. Powell*
ROSSANO, his friend	*Mr. Baily*

Women

CALISTA, daughter to Sciolto	*Mrs. Barry*
LAVINIA, sister to Altamont and wife to Horatio	*Mrs. Bracegirdle*
LUCILLA, confidante to Calista	*Mrs. Prince*

SERVANTS TO SCIOLTO

SCENE, *Sciolto's palace and garden, with some part of the street near it, in Genoa*

The Fair Penitent

ACT I

SCENE, *a garden belonging to Sciolto's palace.*
Enter Altamont *and* Horatio.

ALTAMONT.

    Let this auspicious day be ever sacred,
    No mourning, no misfortunes happen on it;
    Let it be marked for triumphs and rejoicings;
    Let happy lovers ever make it holy,
    Choose it to bless their hopes and crown their wishes,   5
    This happy day that gives me my Calista.

HORATIO.

    Yes, Altamont, today thy better stars
    Are joined to shed their kindest influence on thee;
    Sciolto's noble hand, that raised thee first,
    Half dead and drooping o'er thy father's grave,   10
    Completes its bounty and restores thy name
    To that high rank and luster which it boasted
    Before ungrateful Genoa had forgot
    The merit of thy godlike father's arms;
    Before that country which he long had served   15
    In watchful councils and in winter camps
    Had cast off his white age to want and wretchedness,
    And made their court to faction by his ruin.

ALTAMONT.

    O great Sciolto! O my more than father!
    Let me not live but at thy very name   20
    My eager heart springs up and leaps with joy.
    When I forget the vast, vast debt I owe thee,

---

18. *And . . . ruin.*] ruined the father in order to gain favor with a court faction.

Forget! (but 'tis impossible) then let me
Forget the use and privilege of reason,
Be driven from the commerce of mankind   25
To wander in the desert among brutes,
To bear the various fury of the seasons,
The night's unwholesome dew and noonday's heat,
To be the scorn of earth and curse of heav'n.

HORATIO.

So open, so unbounded was his goodness,   30
It reached ev'n me, because I was thy friend.
When that great man I loved, thy noble father,
Bequeathed thy gentle sister to my arms,
His last dear pledge and legacy of friendship,
That happy tie made me Sciolto's son;   35
He called us his, and with a parent's fondness
Indulged us in his wealth, blessed us with plenty,
Healed all our cares, and sweetened love itself.

ALTAMONT.

By heav'n, he found my fortunes so abandoned
That nothing but a miracle could raise 'em;   40
My father's bounty and the state's ingratitude
Had stripped him bare, nor left him ev'n a grave;
Undone myself, and sinking with his ruin,
I had no wealth to bring, nothing to succor him
But fruitless tears.

HORATIO.   Yet what thou couldst thou didst,   45
And didst it like a son; when his hard creditors,
Urged and assisted by Lothario's father
(Foe to thy house and rival of their greatness),
By sentence of the cruel law, forbid
His venerable corpse to rest in earth,   50
Thou gav'st thyself a ransom for his bones;
With piety uncommon didst give up
Thy hopeful youth to slaves who ne'er knew mercy,
Sour, unrelenting, money-loving villains
Who laugh at human nature and forgiveness,   55
And are like fiends, the factors for destruction.
Heav'n, who beheld the pious act, approved it,
And bade Sciolto's bounty be its proxy,
To bless thy filial virtue with abundance.

ALTAMONT.

But see he comes, the author of my happiness,   60
The man who saved my life from deadly sorrow,
Who bids my days be blessed with peace and plenty,
And satisfies my soul with love and beauty.

Enter Sciolto; *he runs to* Altamont *and embraces him.*

SCIOLTO.

Joy to thee, Altamont! Joy to myself!
Joy to this happy morn that makes thee mine,   65
That kindly grants what nature had denied me,
And makes me father of a son like thee.

ALTAMONT.

My father! O, let me unlade my breast,
Pour out the fullness of my soul before you,
Show ev'ry tender, ev'ry grateful thought   70
This wond'rous goodness stirs. But 'tis impossible,
And utterance all is vile, since I can only
Swear you reign here, but never tell how much.

SCIOLTO.

It is enough; I know thee—thou art honest;
Goodness innate and worth hereditary   75
Are in thy mind; thy noble father's virtues
Spring freshly forth and blossom in thy youth.

ALTAMONT.

Thus heav'n from nothing raised his fair creation,
And then with wond'rous joy beheld its beauty,
Well pleased to see the excellence he gave.   80

SCIOLTO.

O noble youth! I swear since first I knew thee,
Ev'n from that day of sorrows when I saw thee,
Adorned and lovely in thy filial tears,
The mourner and redeemer of thy father,
I set thee down and sealed thee for my own;   85
Thou art my son, ev'n near me as Calista.
Horatio and Lavinia too are mine;   *Embraces* Horatio.
All are my children, and shall share my heart.
But wherefore waste we thus this happy day?
The laughing minutes summon thee to joy,   90
And with new pleasures court thee as they pass;
Thy waiting bride ev'n chides thee for delaying,

And swears thou com'st not with a bridegroom's haste.

ALTAMONT.
 O, could I hope there was one thought of Altamont,
 One kind remembrance in Calista's breast,   95
 The winds, with all their wings, would be too slow
 To bear me to her feet. For, O, my father,
 Amidst this stream of joy that bears me on,
 Blessed as I am and honored in your friendship,
 There is one pain that hangs upon my heart.   100

SCIOLTO.
 What means my son?

ALTAMONT.   When, at your intercession,
 Last night Calista yielded to my happiness,
 Just ere we parted, as I sealed my vows
 With rapture on her lips, I found her cold,
 As a dead lover's statue on his tomb;   105
 A rising storm of passion shook her breast,
 Her eyes a piteous show'r of tears let fall,
 And then she sighed as if her heart were breaking.
 With all the tend'rest eloquence of love
 I begged to be a sharer in her grief;   110
 But she, with looks averse and eyes that froze me,
 Sadly replied, her sorrows were her own,
 Nor in a father's pow'r to dispose of.

SCIOLTO.
 Away! It is the cozenage of their sex,
 One of the common arts they practice on us,   115
 To sigh and weep then when their hearts beat high
 With expectation of the coming joy;
 Thou hast in camps and fighting fields been bred,
 Unknowing in the subtleties of women;
 The virgin bride who swoons with deadly fear   120
 To see the end of all her wishes near,
 When, blushing, from the light and public eyes
 To the kind covert of the night she flies,
 With equal fires to meet the bridegroom moves,
 Melts in his arms, and with a loose she loves. *Exeunt.* 125

Enter Lothario *and* Rossano.

LOTHARIO.
 The father and the husband!

ROSSANO.   Let them pass,
    They saw us not.
LOTHARIO.   I care not if they did;
    Ere long I mean to meet 'em face to face
    And gall 'em with my triumph o'er Calista.
ROSSANO.
    You loved her once.
LOTHARIO.   I liked her, would have married her,   130
    But that it pleased her father to refuse me,
    To make this honorable fool her husband.
    For which, if I forget him, may the shame
    I mean to brand his name with, stick on mine.
ROSSANO.
    She, gentle soul, was kinder than her father.   135
LOTHARIO.
    She was, and oft in private gave me hearing,
    Till, by long list'ning to the soothing tale,
    At length her easy heart was wholly mine.
ROSSANO.
    I have heard you oft describe her, haughty, insolent,
    And fierce with high disdain; it moves my wonder   140
    That virtue thus defended should be yielded
    A pray to loose desires.
LOTHARIO.   Hear, then, I'll tell thee.
    Once in a lone and secret hour of night,
    When ev'ry eye was closed, and the pale moon
    And stars alone shone conscious of the theft,   145
    Hot with the Tuscan grape and high in blood,
    Hap'ly I stole unheeded to her chamber.
ROSSANO.
    That minute sure was lucky.
LOTHARIO.   O 'twas great.
    I found the fond, believing, love-sick maid
    Loose, unattired, warm, tender, full of wishes;   150
    Fierceness and pride, the guardians of her honor,
    Were charmed to rest, and love alone was waking.
    Within her rising bosom all was calm

142. Hear, then,] *MJ*; Hear, then
Q, D1-3.

As peaceful seas that know no storms and only
Are gently lifted up and down by tides.   155
I snatched the glorious, golden opportunity,
And with prevailing, youthful ardor pressed her,
Till with short sighs and murmuring reluctance
The yielding fair one gave me perfect happiness.
Ev'n all the livelong night we passed in bliss,   160
In ecstasies too fierce to last forever;
At length the morn and cold indifference came;
When fully sated with the luscious banquet,
I hastily took leave and left the nymph
To think on what was past, and sigh alone.   165

ROSSANO.
    You saw her soon again.

LOTHARIO.   Too soon I saw her;
    For, O, that meeting was not like the former;
    I found my heart no more beat high with transport,
    No more I sighed and languished for enjoyment;
    'Twas past, and reason took her turn to reign,   170
    While ev'ry weakness fell before her throne.

ROSSANO.
    What of the lady?

LOTHARIO.   With uneasy fondness
    She hung upon me, wept, and sighed, and swore
    She was undone, talked of a priest and marriage,
    Of flying with me from her father's pow'r,   175
    Called ev'ry saint and blessed angel down
    To witness for her that she was my wife.
    I started at that name.

ROSSANO.   What answer made you?

LOTHARIO.
    None; but pretending sudden pain and illness,
    Escaped the persecution; two nights since,   180
    By message urged, and frequent importunity,
    Again I saw her. Straight with tears and sighs,
    With swelling breasts, with swooning, with distraction,
    With all the subtleties and pow'rful arts
    Of willful woman lab'ring for her purpose,   185
    Again she told the same dull, nauseous tale.
    Unmoved, I begged her spare th'ungrateful subject,

Since I resolved, that love and peace of mind
Might flourish long inviolate betwixt us,
Never to load it with the marriage chain;   190
That I would still retain her in my heart,
My ever gentle mistress and my friend;
But for those other names of wife and husband,
They only meant ill nature, cares, and quarrels.

ROSSANO.

How bore she this reply?

LOTHARIO.   Ev'n as the earth   195
When (winds pent up or eating fires beneath,
Shaking the mass) she labors with destruction.
At first her rage was dumb and wanted words,
But when the storm found way, 'twas wild and loud.
Mad as the priestess of the Delphic god,   200
Enthusiastic passion swelled her breast,
Enlarged her voice, and ruffled all her form;
Proud, and disdainful of the love I proffered,
She called me "Villain! Monster! Base betrayer!"
At last, in very bitterness of soul,   205
With deadly imprecations on herself,
She vowed severely ne'er to see me more,
Then bid me fly that minute; I obeyed,
And, bowing, left her to grow cool at leisure.

ROSSANO.

She has relented since, else why this message   210
To meet the keeper of her secrets here
This morning?

LOTHARIO.   See the person whom you named.

Enter Lucilla.

Well, my ambassadress, what must we treat of?
Come you to menace war and proud defiance,
Or does the peaceful olivè grace your message?   215
Is your fair mistress calmer? Does she soften?

204. Base betrayer!] *MJ*; Base!
Betrayer! *Q, D1–3.*.

200–201. *Mad . . . breast*] The priestess of Apollo at the oracle at Delphi
gave her replies to questions in an ecstatic voice; she was "enthusiastic"
in the Greek sense of being possessed by the god.

And must we love again? Perhaps she means
To treat in juncture with her new ally,
And make her husband party to th'agreement.

LUCILLA.

Is this well done, my lord? Have you put off   220
All sense of human nature? Keep a little,
A little pity to distinguish manhood,
Lest other men, though cruel, should disclaim you,
And judge you to be numbered with the brutes.

LOTHARIO.

I see thou'st learned to rail.

LUCILLA.   I've learned to weep;   225
That lesson my sad mistress often gives me;
By day she seeks some melancholy shade
To hide her sorrows from the prying world;
At night she watches all the long, long hours,
And listens to the winds and beating rain,   230
With sighs as loud and tears that fall as fast.
Then ever and anon she wrings her hands,
And cries, "False, false Lothario!"

LOTHARIO.   O, no more!
I swear thou'lt spoil thy pretty face with crying,
And thou hast beauty that may make thy fortune;   235
Some keeping cardinal shall dote upon thee,
And barter his church treasure for thy freshness.

LUCILLA.

What! Shall I sell my innocence and youth
For wealth or titles to perfidious man!
To man, who makes his mirth of our undoing!   240
The base, professed betrayer of our sex!
Let me grow old in all misfortunes else,
Rather than know the sorrows of Calista.

LOTHARIO.

Does she send thee to chide in her behalf?
I swear thou dost it with so good a grace   245
That I could almost love thee for thy frowning.

LUCILLA.

Read there, my lord, there, in her own sad lines,

Giving a letter.

Which best can tell the story of her woes,
That grief of heart which your unkindness gives her.

LOTHARIO (*reads*).

    "Your cruelty—obedience to my father—give my hand to 250
Altamont."
    (*Aside.*) By heav'n, 'tis well; such ever be the gifts
With which I greet the man whom my soul hates.
But to go on!
    "—Wish—heart—honor—too faithless—weakness—to- 255
morrow—last trouble—lost Calista."
Women, I see, can change as well as men;
She writes me here, forsaken as I am,
That I should bind my brows with mournful willow,
For she has given her hand to Altamont.   260
Yet tell the fair inconstant—

LUCILLA.   How, my lord?

LOTHARIO.

    Nay, no more angry words; say to Calista,
The humblest of her slaves shall wait her pleasure,
If she can leave her happy husband's arms
To think upon so lost a thing as I am.   265

LUCILLA.

    Alas! For pity come with gentler looks;
Wound not her heart with this unmanly triumph;
And though you love her not, yet swear you do,
So shall dissembling once be virtuous in you.

LOTHARIO.

    Ha! Who comes here?

LUCILLA.   The bridegroom's friend, Horatio. 270
He must not see us here; tomorrow early
Be at the garden gate.

LOTHARIO.   Bear to my love
My kindest thought, and swear I will not fail her.

    Lothario, *putting up the letter hastily, drops it as he goes out.*
          Exeunt Lothario *and* Rossano *one way,* Lucilla *another.*

Enter Horatio.

HORATIO.

    Sure 'tis the very error of my eyes:
Waking I dream, or I beheld Lothario;   275
He seemed conferring with Calista's woman;

At my approach they started, and retired.
What business could he have here, and with her?
I know he bears the noble Altamont
Professed and deadly hate— What paper's this?   280
Taking up the letter.

Ha! To Lothario—'sdeath! Calista's name!   *Opening it.*
Confusion and misfortune!   *Reads.*
"Your cruelty has at length determined me, and I have
resolved this morning to yield a perfect obedience to my
father and to give my hand to Altamont, in spite of my 285
weakness for the false Lothario. I could almost wish I had
that heart and that honor to bestow with it which you have
robbed me of—"
Damnation! To the test—   *Reads again.*
"But, O, I fear, could I retrieve 'em I should again be 290
undone by the too faithless, yet too lovely Lothario; this is
the last weakness of my pen, and tomorrow shall be the last
in which I will indulge my eyes. Lucilla shall conduct you,
if you are kind enough to let me see you; it shall be the last
trouble you shall meet with from   295
                              The lost Calista."
The lost indeed! For thou art gone as far
As there can be perdition. Fire and sulphur,
Hell is the sole avenger of such crimes.
O that the ruin were but all thy own!   300
Thou wilt ev'n make thy father curse his age;
At sight of this black scroll the gentle Altamont
(For, O, I know his heart is set upon thee)
Shall droop and hang his discontented head,
Like merit scorned by insolent authority,   305
And never grace the public with his virtues.—
Perhaps ev'n now he gazes fondly on her,
And, thinking soul and body both alike,
Blesses the perfect workmanship of heav'n;
Then sighing, to his ev'ry care speaks peace,   310
And bids his heart be satisfied with happiness.
O wretched husband! While she hangs about thee
With idle blandishments and plays the fond one,
Ev'n then her hot imagination wanders,

Contriving riot and loose scapes of love;   315
And while she claps thee close, makes thee a monster.
What if I give this paper to her father?
It follows that his justice dooms her dead,
And breaks his heart with sorrow; hard return
For all the good his hand has heaped on us.   320
Hold, let me take a moment's thought.

Enter Lavinia.

LAVINIA.   My lord!
Trust me, it joys my heart that I have found you.
Enquiring wherefore you had left the company
Before my brother's nuptial rites were ended,
They told me you had felt some sudden illness.   325
Where are you sick? Is it your head? your heart?
Tell me, my love, and ease my anxious thoughts,
That I may take you gently in my arms,
Soothe you to rest, and soften all your pains.

HORATIO.
It were unjust; no, let me spare my friend,   330
Lock up the fatal secret in my breast,
Nor tell him that which will undo his quiet.

LAVINIA.
What means my lord?

HORATIO.   Ha! Saidst thou, my Lavinia?

LAVINIA.
Alas, you know not what you make me suffer.
Why are you pale? Why did you start and tremble?   335
Whence is that sigh? And wherefore are your eyes
Severely raised to heav'n? The sick man thus,
Acknowledging the summons of his fate,
Lifts up his feeble hands and eyes for mercy,
And with confusion thinks upon his audit.   340

HORATIO.
O, no! Thou hast mistook my sickness quite;
These pangs are of the soul. Would I had met
Sharpest convulsions, spotted pestilences,
Or any other deadly foe to life,

---

316. *monster*] cuckold, a horned man.

Rather than heave beneath this load of thought.   345

LAVINIA.

    Alas, what is it? Wherefore turn you from me?
    Why did you falsely call me your Lavinia,
    And swear I was Horatio's better half,
    Since now you mourn unkindly by yourself,
    And rob me of my partnership of sadness?   350
    Witness, you holy pow'rs, who know my truth,
    There cannot be a chance in life so miserable,
    Nothing so very hard but I could bear it
    Much rather than my love should treat me coldly,
    And use me like a stranger to his heart.   355

HORATIO.

    Seek not to know what I would hide from all,
    But most from thee. I never knew a pleasure,
    Aught that was joyful, fortunate, or good,
    But straight I ran to bless thee with the tidings,
    And laid up all my happiness with thee;   360
    But wherefore, wherefore should I give thee pain?
    Then spare me, I conjure thee, ask no further;
    Allow my melancholy thoughts this privilege,
    And let 'em brood in secret o'er their sorrows.

LAVINIA.

    It is enough; chide not, and all is well;   365
    Forgive me if I saw you sad, Horatio,
    And asked to weep out part of your misfortunes;
    I wo' not press to know what you forbid me.
    Yet, my loved lord, yet you must grant me this:
    Forget your cares for this one happy day,   370
    Devote this day to mirth and to your Altamont;
    For his dear sake let peace be in your looks.
    Ev'n now the jocund bridegroom wants your wishes;
    He thinks the priest has but half blessed his marriage
    Till his friend hails him with the sound of joy.   375

HORATIO.

    O, never, never, never! Thou art innocent;
    Simplicity from ill, pure native truth,
    And candor of the mind adorn thee ever;
    But there are such, such false ones in the world,
    'Twould fill they gentle soul with wild amazement   380

To hear their story told.

LAVINIA.   False ones, my lord?

HORATIO.

Fatally fair they are, and in their smiles
The graces, little loves, and young desires inhabit;
But all that gaze upon 'em are undone,
For they are false, luxurious in their appetites,   385
And all the heav'n they hope for is variety;
One lover to another still succeeds,
Another, and another after that,
And the last fool is welcome as the former,
Till, having loved his hour out, he gives place,   390
And mingles with the herd that went before him.

LAVINIA.

Can there be such? And have they peace of mind?
Have they in all the series of their changing
One happy hour? If women are such things,
How was I formed so different from my sex?   395
My little heart is satisfied with you;
You take up all her room, as in a cottage
Which harbors some benighted princely stranger,
Where the good man, proud of his hospitality,
Yields all his homely dwelling to his guest,   400
And hardly keeps a corner to himself.

HORATIO.

O, were they all like thee, men would adore 'em,
And all the business of their lives be loving;
The nuptial band should be the pledge of peace,
And all domestic cares and quarrels cease;   405
The world should learn to love by virtuous rules,
And marriage be no more the jest of fools.   *Exeunt.*

End of the First Act.

ACT II

SCENE, *a hall.*
Enter Calista *and* Lucilla.

CALISTA.

    Be dumb forever, silent as the grave,
    Nor let thy fond, officious love disturb
    My solemn sadness with the sound of joy.
    If thou wilt soothe me, tell some dismal tale
    Of pining discontent and black despair;   5
    For, O, I've gone around through all my thoughts,
    But all are indignation, love, or shame,
    And my dear peace of mind is lost forever.

LUCILLA.

    Why do you follow still that wand'ring fire
    That has misled your weary steps and leaves you   10
    Benighted in a wilderness of woe?
    That false Lothario! Turn from the deceiver;
    Turn, and behold where gentle Altamont,
    Kind as the softest virgin of our sex,
    And faithful as the simple village swain   15
    That never knew the courtly vice of changing,
    Sighs at your feet and woos you to be happy.

CALISTA.

    Away—I think not of him. My sad soul
    Has formed a dismal, melancholy scene,
    Such a retreat as I would wish to find;   20
    An unfrequented vale, o'ergrown with trees
    Mossy and old, within whose lonesome shade
    Ravens and birds ill-omened only dwell;
    No sound to break the silence but a brook
    That, bubbling, winds among the weeds; no mark   25
    Of any human shape that had been there,
    Unless a skeleton of some poor wretch
    Who had long since, like me, by love undone,
    Sought that sad place out to despair and die in.

LUCILLA.

    Alas for pity!

CALISTA.   There I fain would hide me   30

From the base world, from malice, and from shame;
For 'tis the solemn counsel of my soul
Never to live with public loss of honor;
'Tis fixed to die, rather than bear the insolence
Of each affected she that tells my story,   35
And blesses her good stars that she is virtuous.
To be a tale for fools! Scorned by the women,
And pitied by the men! O, insupportable!

LUCILLA.

Can you perceive the manifest destruction,
The gaping gulf that opens just before you,   40
And yet rush on, though conscious of the danger?
O, hear me, hear your ever faithful creature;
By all the good I wish, by all the ill
My trembling heart forebodes, let me entreat you
Never to see this faithless man again;   45
Let me forbid his coming.

CALISTA.   On thy life
I charge thee, no; my genius drives me on;
I must, I will behold him once again;
Perhaps it is the crisis of my fate,
And this one interview shall end my cares.   50
My lab'ring heart, that swells with indignation,
Heaves to discharge the burden; that once done,
The busy thing shall rest within its cell,
And never beat again.

LUCILLA.   Trust not to that;
Rage is the shortest passion of our souls;   55
Like narrow brooks that rise with sudden show'rs,
It swells in haste, and falls again as soon;
Still as it ebbs, the softer thoughts flow in,
And the deceiver, love, supplies its place.

CALISTA.

I have been wronged enough to arm my temper   60
Against the smooth delusion; but alas!
(Chide not my weakness, gentle maid, but pity me),
A woman's softness hangs about me still;
Then let me blush, and tell thee all my folly.
I swear I could not see the dear betrayer   65
Kneel at my feet and sigh to be forgiven,

But my relenting heart would pardon all,
And quite forget 'twas he that had undone me.

LUCILLA.

Ye sacred powers, whose gracious providence
Is watchful for our good, guard me from men,   70
From their deceitful tongues, their vows and flatteries;
Still let me pass neglected by their eyes,
Let my bloom wither and my form decay,
That none may think it worth his while to ruin me,
And fatal love may never be my bane.   75

CALISTA.

Ha! Altamont? Calista, now be wary,
And guard thy soul's accesses with dissembling;
Nor let this hostile husband's eyes explore
The warring passions and tumultuous thoughts
That rage within thee and deform thy reason.   80

Enter Altamont.

ALTAMONT.

Be gone, my cares, I give you to the winds,
Far to be borne, far from the happy Altamont;
For from this sacred era of my love
A better order of succeeding days
Come smiling forward, white and lucky all.   85
Calista is the mistress of the year;
She crowns the seasons with auspicious beauty,
And bids ev'n all my hours be good and joyful.

CALISTA.

If I was ever mistress of such happiness,
O, wherefore did I play th'unthrifty fool,   90
And, wasting all on others, leave myself
Without one thought of joy to give me comfort?

ALTAMONT.

O mighty Love! Shall that fair face profane
This thy great festival with frowns and sadness!
I swear it sha' not be, for I will woo thee   95

---

85. *white and lucky*] A fortunate day was marked by the Romans with a
white stone. Cf. Catullus, LXVIII, 1. 148: "... *quem lapide illa, diem,
candidiore notat*": the day which she marks with a whiter stone.

With sighs so moving, with so warm a transport
That thou shalt catch the gentle flame from me,
And kindle into joy.
CALISTA.　　　　　　　I tell thee, Altamont,
　Such hearts as ours were never paired above;
　Ill suited to each other; joined, not matched;　　　　100
　Some sullen influence, a foe to both,
　Has wrought this fatal marriage to undo us.
　Mark but the frame and temper of our minds,
　How very much we differ. Ev'n this day,
　That fills thee with such ecstasy and transport,　　　105
　To me brings nothing that should make me bless it,
　Or think it better than the day before,
　Or any other in the course of time
　That dully took its turn and was forgotten.
ALTAMONT.
　If to behold thee as my pledge of happiness,　　　　110
　To know none fair, none excellent beside thee,
　If still to love thee with unwearied constancy,
　Through ev'ry season, ev'ry change of life,
　Through wrinkled age, through sickness and misfortune,
　Be worth the least return of grateful love,　　　　115
　O, then let my Calista bless this day,
　And set it down for happy.
CALISTA.　　　　　　　　'Tis the day
　In which my father gave my hand to Altamont;
　As such I will remember it forever.

　　　　　Enter Sciolto, Horatio, *and* Lavinia.

SCIOLTO.
　Let mirth go on, let pleasure know no pause,　　　　120
　But fill up ev'ry minute of this day.
　'Tis yours, my children, sacred to your loves;
　The glorious sun himself for you looks gay;
　He shines for Altamont and for Calista.
　Let there be music; let the master touch　　　　　125
　The sprightly string and softly breathing flute
　Till harmony rouse ev'ry gentle passion,

101. influence] *D1–3*; inflence *Q*.

Teach the cold maid to lose her fears in love,
And the fierce youth to languish at her feet.
Begin. Ev'n age itself is cheered with music;   130
It wakes a glad remembrance of our youth,
Calls back past joys, and warms us into transport.

Here an entertainment of music and dancing.

SONG

By Mr. Congreve

I

Ah, stay! Ah, turn! Ah, whither would you fly,
    Too charming, too relentless maid?
I follow not to conquer but to die;   135
    You of the fearful are afraid.

II

In vain I call; for she, like fleeting air
    When pressed by some tempestuous wind,
Flies swifter from the voice of my despair,
    Nor casts one pitying look behind.   140

SCIOLTO.

Take care my gates are open, bid all welcome;
All who rejoice with me today are friends;
Let each indulge his genius, each be glad,
Jocund, and free, and swell the feast with mirth.
The sprightly bowl shall cheerfully go round,   145
None shall be grave, nor too severely wise;
Losses and disappointments, cares and poverty,
The rich man's insolence and great man's scorn,
In wine shall be forgotten all. Tomorrow
Will be too soon to think, and to be wretched.   150
O, grant, ye powers, that I may see these happy,
                    Pointing to Altamont *and* Calista.
Completely blest, and I have life enough;
And leave the rest indifferently to fate.   *Exeunt. Manet* Horatio.

HORATIO.

'What if, while all are here intent on reveling,
I privately went forth and sought Lothario?   155
This letter may be forged; perhaps the wantonness

–25–

Of his vain youth, to stain a lady's fame;
Perhaps his malice, to disturb my friend.
O, no! My heart forebodes it must be true.
Methought ev'n now I marked the starts of guilt   160
That shook her soul, though damned dissimulation
Screened her dark thoughts, and set to public view
A specious face of innocence and beauty.
O, false appearance! What is all our sovereignty,
Our boasted pow'r? When they oppose their arts,   165
Still they prevail, and we are found their fools.
With such smooth looks and many a gentle word
The first fair she beguiled her easy lord;
Too blind with love and beauty to beware,
He fell unthinking in the fatal snare;   170
Nor could believe that such a heav'nly face
Had bargained with the devil to damn her wretched race. *Exit.*

[II.ii]   SCENE, *the street near Sciolto's palace.*
                 Enter Lothario *and* Rossano.

LOTHARIO.

To tell thee, then, the purport of my thoughts,
The loss of this fond paper would not give me
A moment of disquiet were it not
My instrument of vengeance on this Altamont;
Therefore I mean to wait some opportunity   5
Of speaking with the maid we saw this morning.

ROSSANO.

I wish you, sir, to think upon the danger
Of being seen; today their friends are round 'em,
And any eye that lights by chance on you
Shall put your life and safety to the hazard.   10
                                    They confer aside.

                 Enter Horatio.

HORATIO.

Still I must doubt some mystery of mischief,

163. specious] *Q, D1–2*; spacious
D3.

---

11. *doubt*] suspeçt.

Some artifice beneath; Lothario's father—
I knew him well; he was sagacious, cunning,
Fluent in words, and bold in peaceful councils,
But of a cold, unactive hand in war.   15
Yet with these coward's virtues he undid
My unsuspecting, valiant, honest friend.
This son, if fame mistakes not, is more hot,
More open, and unartful. Ha! He's here!   *Seeing him.*

LOTHARIO.
   Damnation! He again! This second time   20
   Today he has crossed me like my evil genius.

HORATIO.
   I sought you, sir.
LOTHARIO.   'Tis well then I am found.

HORATIO.
   'Tis well you are. The man who wrongs my friend
   To the earth's utmost verge I would pursue;
   No place, though e'er so holy, should protect him;   25
   No shape that artful fear e'er formed should hide him,
   Till he fair answer made, and did me justice.

LOTHARIO.
   Ha! Dost thou know me, that I am Lothario?
   As great a name as this proud city boasts of.
   Who is this mighty man, then, this Horatio,   30
   That I should basely hide me from his anger,
   Lest he should chide me for his friend's displeasure?

HORATIO.
   The brave, 'tis true, do never shun the light;
   Just are their thoughts, and open are their tempers,
   Freely without disguise they love and hate,   35
   Still are they found in the fair face of day,
   And heav'n and men are judges of their actions.

LOTHARIO.
   Such let 'em be of mine; there's not a purpose
   Which my soul ever framed or my hand acted,
   But I could well have bid the world look on,   40
   And what I once durst do, have dared to justify.

HORATIO.
   Where was this open boldness, this free spirit,
   When but this very morning I surprised thee

In base, dishonest privacy, consulting
And bribing a poor, mercenary wretch 45
To sell her lady's secrets, stain her honor,
And with a forged contrivance blast her virtue?
At sight of me thou fled'st!

LOTHARIO. Ha! Fled from thee?

HORATIO.

Thou fled'st, and guilt was on thee; like a thief,
A pilferer descried in some dark corner, 50
Who there had lodged with mischievous intent
To rob and ravage at the hour of rest,
And do a midnight murder on the sleepers.

LOTHARIO.

Slave! Villain! *Offers to draw:* Rossano *holds him.*

ROSSAÑO. Hold, my lord! Think where you are,
Think how unsafe and hurtful to your honor 55
It were to urge a quarrel in this place,
And shock the peaceful city with a broil.

LOTHARIO.

Then since thou dost provoke my vengeance, know
I would not for this city's worth, for all
Which the sea wafts to our Ligurian shore, 60
But that the joys I reaped with that fond wanton,
The wife of Altamont, should be as public
As is the noonday sun, air, earth, or water,
Or any common benefit of nature.
Think'st thou I meant the shame should be concealed? 65
O, no! By hell and vengeance, all I wanted
Was some fit messenger to bear the news
To the dull, doting husband; now I have found him,
And thou art he.

HORATIO. I hold thee base enough
To break through law, and spurn at sacred order, 70
And do a brutal injury like this;
Yet mark me well, young lord, I think Calista
Too nice, too noble, and too great of soul
To be the prey of such a thing as thou art.
'Twas base and poor, unworthy of a man, 75
To forge a scroll so villainous and loose,
And mark it with a noble lady's name;

These are the mean, dishonest arts of cowards,
Strangers to manhood and to glorious dangers,
Who, bred at home in idleness and riot,   80
Ransack for mistresses th'unwholesome stews,
And never know the worth of virtuous love.

LOTHARIO.

Think'st thou I forged the letter? Think so still,
Till the broad shame comes staring in thy face,
And boys shall hoot the cuckold as he passes.   85

HORATIO.

Away—no woman could descend so low;
A skipping, dancing, worthless tribe you are;
Fit only for yourselves, you herd together;
And when the circling glass warms your vain hearts,
You talk of beauties that you never saw   90
And fancy raptures that you never knew.
Legends of saints who never yet had being,
Or, being, ne'er were saints, are not so false
As the fond tales which you reccunt of love.

LOTHARIO.

But that I do not hold it worth my leisure,   95
I could produce such damning proof—

HORATIO.   'Tis false!
You blast the fair with lies because they scorn you,
Hate you like age, like ugliness and impotence;
Rather than make you blest, they would die virgins,
And stop the propagation of mankind.   100

LOTHARIO.

It is the curse of fools to be secure,
And that be thine and Altamont's. Dream on,
Nor think upon my vengeance till thou feel'st it.

HORATIO.

Hold, sir, another word, and then farewell.
Though I think greatly of Calista's virtue,   105
And hold it far beyond thy pow'r to hurt,
Yet as she shares the honor of my Altamont,
That treasure of a soldier, bought with blood,
And kept at life's expense, I must not have

88. you] *D1–3*; your *Q*.

(Mark me, young sir) her very name profaned.   110
Learn to restrain the license of your speech;
'Tis held you are too lavish. When you are met
Among your set of fools, talk of your dress,
Of dice, of whores, of horses, and yourselves;
'Tis safer, and becomes your understandings.   115

LOTHARIO.

What if we pass beyond this solemn order,
And, in defiance of the stern Horatio,
Indulge our gayer thoughts, let laughter loose,
And use his sacred friendship for our mirth?

HORATIO.

'Tis well! Sir, you are pleasant—

LOTHARIO.   By the joys   120
Which yet my soul has uncontrolled pursued,
I would not turn aside from my least pleasure
Though all thy force were armed to bar my way;
But like the birds, great Nature's happy commoners,
That haunt in woods, in meads, in flow'ry gardens,   125
Rifle the sweets, and taste her choicest fruits,
Yet scorn to ask the lordly owners leave.

HORATIO.

What liberty has vain, presumptuous youth,
That thou shouldst dare provoke me unchastised?
But henceforth, boy, I warn thee, shun my walks;   130
If in the bounds of yon forbidden place
Again thou'rt found, expect a punishment
Such as great souls, impatient of an injury,
Exact from those who wrong 'em much, ev'n death,
Or something worse; an injured husband's vengeance   135
Shall print a thousand wounds, tear thy fine form,
And scatter thee to all the winds of heav'n.

LOTHARIO.

Is then my way in Genoa prescribed
By a dependent on the wretched Altamont,
A talking sir that brawls for him in taverns,   140
And vouches for his valor's reputation?

123. way] *Q, D1–2*; ways *D3*.

HORATIO.

    Away—thy speech is fouler than thy manners.

LOTHARIO.

    Or if there be a name more vile, his parasite,

    A beggar's parasite!

HORATIO.   Now learn humanity,

                Offers to strike him; Rossano *interposes.*

    Since brutes and boys are only taught with blows.   145

LOTHARIO.

    Damnation!   *They draw.*

ROSSANO.   Hold, this goes no further here.

    Horatio, 'tis too much; already see

    The crowd are gath'ring to us.

LOTHARIO.   O, Rossano!

    Or give me way, or thou'rt no more my friend.

ROSSANO.

    Sciolto's servants too have ta'en the alarm;   150

    You'll be oppressed by numbers; be advised,

    Or I must force you hence; take't on my word,

    You shall have justice done you on Horatio.

    Put up, my lord.

LOTHARIO.   This wo' not brook delay;

    West of the town a mile, among the rocks,   155

    Two hours ere noon tomorrow I expect thee,

    Thy single hand to mine.

HORATIO.   I'll meet thee there.

LOTHARIO.

    Tomorrow, O my better stars! Tomorrow

    Exert your influence, shine strongly for me;

    'Tis not a common conquest I would gain,   160

    Since love, as well as arms, must grace my triumph.

                    Exeunt Lothario *and* Rossano.

HORATIO.

    Two hours ere noon tomorrow! Ha! Ere that

    He sees Calista! O unthinking fool—

    What if I urged her with the crime and danger?

    If any spark from heav'n remain unquenched   165

150. the alarm] *Q*; th'alarm *D1–3.*

Within her breast, my breath perhaps may wake it;
Could I but prosper there, I would not doubt
My combat with that loud, vainglorious boaster.
Were you, ye fair, but cautious whom ye trust,
Did you but think how seldom fools are just,   170
So many of your sex would not in vain
Of broken vows and faithless men complain.
Of all the various wretches love has made,
How few have been by men of sense betrayed?
Convinced by reason, they your pow'r confess,   ⎫   175
Pleased to be happy, as you're pleased to bless,   ⎬
And conscious of your worth, can never love you less.⎭   *Exit.*

End of the Second Act.

177. S.D. *Exit.*] *Q, D1–2; Exeunt
D3.*

ACT III

SCENE, *an apartment in Sciolto's palace.*
Enter Sciolto *and* Calista.

SCIOLTO.

    Now by my life, my honor, 'tis too much.
    Have I not marked thee wayward as thou art,
    Perverse and sullen all this day of joy?
    When ev'ry heart was cheered, and mirth went round,
    Sorrow, displeasure, and repining anguish   5
    Sat on thy brow, like some malignant planet,
    Foe to the harvest and the healthy year,
    Who scowls adverse, and lowers upon the world,
    When all the other stars, with gentle aspect,
    Propitious shine, and meaning good to man.   10

CALISTA.

    Is then the task of duty half performed?
    Has not your daughter giv'n herself to Altamont,
    Yielded the native freedom of her will
    To an imperious husband's lordly rule
    To gratify a father's stern command?   15

SCIOLTO.

    Dost thou complain?

CALISTA.   For pity, do not frown then.
    If in despite of all my vowed obedience,
    A sigh breaks out, or a tear falls by chance;
    For, O, that sorrow which has drawn your anger
    Is the sad native of Calista's breast,   20
    And, once possessed, will never quit its dwelling
    Till life, the prop of all, shall leave the building
    To tumble down and moulder into ruin.

SCIOLTO.

    Now by the sacred dust of that dear saint
    That was thy mother, by her wond'rous goodness,   25
    Her soft, her tender, most complying sweetness,
    I swear some sullen thought that shuns the light
    Lurks underneath that sadness in thy visage.

---

22. prop of all] *D1–3*; prop all *Q*.

But mark me well: though by yon heav'n I love thee
As much, I think, as a fond parent can,　　　　　　　　30
Yet shouldst thou (which the pow'rs above forbid)
E'er stain the honor of thy name with infamy,
I cast thee off as one whose impious hands
Had rent asunder nature's nearest ties,
Which, once divided, never join again.　　　　　　　　35
Today I have made a noble youth thy husband;
Consider well his worth, reward his love,
Be willing to be happy, and thou art so.　　　　　*Exit* Sciolto.

CALISTA.

How hard is the condition of our sex,
Through ev'ry state of life the slaves of man!　　　　　40
In all the dear, delightful days of youth
A rigid father dictates to our wills,
And deals out pleasure with a scanty hand;
To his, the tyrant husband's reign succeeds;
Proud with opinion of superior reason,　　　　　　　　45
He holds domestic business and devotion
All we are capable to know, and shuts us,
Like cloistered idiots, from the world's acquaintance
And all the joys of freedom; wherefore are we
Born with high souls but to assert ourselves,　　　　　50
Shake off this vile obedience they exact,
And claim an equal empire o'er the world?

Enter Horatio.

HORATIO.

She's here! Yet, O, my tongue is at a loss;
Teach me, some pow'r, that happy art of speech
To dress my purpose up in gracious words,　　　　　　55
Such as may softly steal upon her soul
And never waken the tempestuous passions.
By heav'n, she weeps! —Forgive me, fair Calista,
If I presume, on privilege of friendship,
To join my grief to yours, and mourn the evils　　　　60
That hurt your peace and quench those eyes in tears.

44. succeeds;] *JRS, MJ*; succeeds
Q, *D1–3*.

CALISTA.

    To steal unlooked-for on my private sorrow
    Speaks not the man of honor nor the friend,
    But rather means the spy.

HORATIO.   Unkindly said!

    For, O, as sure as you accuse me falsely,   65
    I come to prove myself Calista's friend.

CALISTA.

    You are my husband's friend, the friend of Altamont.

HORATIO.

    Are you not one? Are you not joined by heav'n,
    Each interwoven with the other's fate?
    Are you not mixed like streams of meeting rivers   70
    Whose blended waters are no more distinguished,
    But roll into the sea, one common flood?
    Then who can give his friendship but to one?
    Who can be Altamont's, and not Calista's?

CALISTA.

    Force, and the wills of our imperious rulers   75
    May bind two bodies in one wretched chain;
    But minds will still look back to their own choice.
    So the poor captive in a foreign realm
    Stands on the shore, and sends his wishes back
    To the dear native land from whence he came.   80

HORATIO.

    When souls that should agree to will the same,
    To have one common object for their wishes,
    Look different ways, regardless of each other,
    Think what a train of wretchedness ensues:
    Love shall be banished from the genial bed,   85
    The nights shall all be lonely and unquiet,
    And ev'ry day shall be a day of cares.

CALISTA.

    Then all the boasted office of thy friendship
    Was but to tell Calista what a wretch she is.
    Alas, what needed that?

HORATIO.   O, rather say   90

    I came to tell her how she might be happy;

86. nights] *Q, D1*; night *D2–3*.

To soothe the secret anguish of her soul,
To comfort that fair mourner, that forlorn one,
And teach her steps to know the paths of peace.

CALISTA.

Say thou to whom this paradise is known,   95
Where lies the blissful region? Mark my way to it,
For, O, 'tis sure, I long to be at rest.

HORATIO.

Then—to be good is to be happy. Angels
Are happier than mankind, because they are better.
Guilt is the source of sorrow; 'tis the fiend,   100
The avenging fiend, that follows us behind
With whips and stings; the blest know none of this,
But rest in everlasting peace of mind,
And find the height of all their heav'n is goodness.

CALISTA.

And what bold parasite's officious tongue   105
Shall dare to tax Calista's name with guilt?

HORATIO.

None should; but 'tis a busy, talking world,
That with licentious breath blows like the wind,
As freely on the palace as the cottage.

CALISTA.

What mystic riddle lurks beneath thy words,   110
Which thou wouldst seem unwilling to express,
As if it meant dishonor to my virtue?
Away with this ambiguous, shuffling phrase,
And let thy oracle be understood.

HORATIO.

Lothario!

CALISTA. Ha! What wouldst thou mean by him? 115

HORATIO.

Lothario and Calista! Thus they join
Two names which heav'n decreed should never meet;
Hence have the talkers of this populous city
A shameful tale to tell for public sport
Of an unhappy beauty, a false fair one   120
Who plighted to a noble youth her faith,
When she had giv'n her honor to a wretch.

CÁLISTA.

    Death and confusion! Have I lived to this?
    Thus to be treated with unmanly insolence!
    To be the sport of a loose ruffian's tongue!   125
    Thus to be used! Thus, like the vilest creature
    That ever was a slave to vice and infamy!

HORATIO.

    By honor and fair truth, you wrong me much,
    For on my soul nothing but strong necessity
    Could urge my tongue to this ungrateful office;   130
    I came with strong reluctance, as if death
    Had stood across my way, to save your honor,
    Yours and Sciolto's, yours and Altamont's,
    Like one who ventures through a burning pile
    To save his tender wife, with all her brood   135
    Of little fondlings, from the dreadful ruin.

CALISTA.

    Is this, is this the famous friend of Altamont,
    For noble worth and deeds of arms renowned?
    Is this, this tale-bearing, officious fellow
    That watches for intelligence from eyes,   140
    This wretched Argus of a jealous husband,
    That fills his easy ears with monstrous tales,
    And makes him toss, and rave, and wreak at length
    Bloody revenge on his defenseless wife,
    Who, guiltless, dies because her fool ran mad?   145

HORATIO.

    Alas, this rage is vain, for if your fame
    Or peace be worth your care, you must be calm,
    And listen to the means are left to save 'em.
    'Tis now the lucky minute of your fate;
    By me your genius speaks, by me it warns you   150
    Never to see that cursed Lothario more,
    Unless you mean to be despised, be shunned
    By all your virtuous maids and noble matrons,
    Unless you have devoted this rare beauty
    To infamy, diseases, prostitution—   155

150. your] *D1–3*; our *Q*.

CALISTA.

    Dishonor blast thee, base, unmannered slave,
    That dar'st forget my birth and sacred sex,
    And shock me with the rude, unhallowed sound!

HORATIO.

    Here kneel, and in the awful face of heav'n
    Breathe out a solemn vow never to see,   160
    Nor think, if possible, on him that ruined thee;
    Or by my Altamont's dear life I swear,
    This paper! —Nay, you must not fly! —This paper,

Holding her.

    This guilty paper shall divulge your shame.

CALISTA.

    What mean'st thou by that paper? What contrivance   165
    Hast thou been forging to deceive my father,
    To turn his heart against his wretched daughter,
    That Altamont and thou may share his wealth?
    A wrong like this will make me ev'n forget
    The weakness of my sex. O for a sword   170
    To urge my vengeance on the villainous hand
    That forged the scroll.

HORATIO.   Behold, can this be forged?
    See where Calista's name—   *Showing the letter near.*

CALISTA.   To atoms thus,   *Tearing it.*
    Thus let me tear the vile, detested falsehood,
    The wicked, lying evidence of shame.   175

HORATIO.

    Confusion!

CALISTA.   Henceforth, thou officious fool,
    Meddle no more, nor dare ev'n on thy life
    To breathe an accent that may touch my virtue;
    I am myself the guardian of my honor,
    And wo' not bear so insolent a monitor.   180

Enter Altamont.

ALTAMONT.

    Where is my life, my love, my charming bride,
    Joy of my heart, and pleasure of my eyes,

171. villainous] Q; villain's D1-3.

The wish, the care, and business of my youth?
O, let me find her, snatch her to my breast,
And tell her she delays my bliss too long,   185
Till my soft soul ev'n sickens with desire.
Disordered—and in tears! Horatio too!
My friend is in amaze! What can it mean?
Tell me, Calista, who has done thee wrong,
That my swift sword may find out the offender,   190
And do thee ample justice.

CALISTA.   Turn to him!

ALTAMONT.

Horatio!

CALISTA.   To that insolent.

ALTAMONT.   My friend!

Could he do this? He, who was half myself!
One faith has ever bound us, and one reason
Guided our wills. Have I not found him just,   195
Honest as truth itself? And could he break
The sanctity of friendship? Could he wound
The heart of Altamont in his Calista?

CALISTA.

I thought what justice I should find from thee!
Go fawn upon him, listen to his tale,   200
Applaud his malice that would blast my fame,
And treat me like a common prostitute.
Thou art perhaps confederate in his mischief,
And wilt believe the legend, if he tells it.

ALTAMONT.

O impious! What presumptuous wretch shall dare   205
To offer at an injury like that?
Priesthood, nor age, nor cowardice itself
Shall save him from the fury of my vengeance.

CALISTA.

The man who dared to do it was Horatio!
Thy darling friend! 'Twas Altamont's Horatio!   210
But mark me well! While thy divided heart
Dotes on a villain that has wronged me thus,
No force shall drag me to thy hated bed;
Nor can my cruel father's pow'r do more
Than shut me in a cloister; there, well pleased,   215

Religious hardships will I learn to bear,
To fast, and freeze at midnight hours of pray'r;
Nor think it hard, within a lonely cell,
With melancholy, speechless saints to dwell,
But bless the day I to that refuge ran,   220
Free from the marriage chain and from that tyrant, man.

Exit Calista.

ALTAMONT.

She's gone; and as she went, ten thousand fires
Shot from her angry eyes, as if she meant
Too well to keep the cruel vow she made.
Now as thou art a man, Horatio, tell me,   225
What means this wild confusion in thy looks,
As if thou wert at variance with thyself,
Madness and reason combating within thee,
And thou wert doubtful which should get the better?

HORATIO.

I would be dumb forever, but thy fate   230
Has otherwise decreed it; thou hast seen
That idol of thy soul, that fair Calista,
Thou hast beheld her tears.

ALTAMONT.   I have seen her weep,
I have seen that lovely one, that dear Calista,
Complaining in the bitterness of sorrow,   235
That thou—my friend, Horatio—thou hadst wronged her!

HORATIO.

That I have wronged her! Had her eyes been fed
From that rich stream which warms her heart, and numbered
For ev'ry falling tear a drop of blood,
It had not been too much; for she has ruined thee,   240
Ev'n thee, my Altamont! She has undone thee.

ALTAMONT.

Dost thou join ruin with Calista's name?
What is so fair, so exquisitely good?
Is she not more than painting can express,
Or youthful poets fancy, when they love?   245
Does she not come, like wisdom or good fortune,
Replete with blessings, giving wealth and honor?
The dowry which she brings is peace and pleasure,
And everlasting joys are in her arms.

HORATIO.

 It had been better thou hadst lived a beggar,   250
 And fed on scraps at great men's surly doors
 Than to have matched with one so false, so fatal—

ALTAMONT.

 It is too much for friendship to allow thee;
 Because I tamely bore the wrong thou didst her,
 Thou dost avow the barb'rous, brutal part,   255
 And urge the injury ev'n to my face.

HORATIO.

 I see she has got possession of thy heart,
 She has charmed thee, like a siren, to her bed,
 With looks of love and with enchanting sounds;
 Too late the rocks and quicksands will appear.   260
 When thou art wrecked upon the faithless shore,
 Then vainly wish thou hadst not left thy friend
 To follow her delusion.

ALTAMONT.   If thy friendship
 Do churlishly deny my love a room,
 It is not worth my keeping; I disclaim it.   265

HORATIO.

 Canst thou so soon forget what I've been to thee?
 I shared the task of nature with thy father,
 And formed with care thy unexperienced youth
 To virtue and to arms.
 Thy noble father, O thou light young man!   270
 Would he have used me thus? One fortune fed us,
 For his was ever mine, mine his, and both
 Together flourished, and together fell.
 He called me friend, like thee; would he have left me
 Thus, for a woman, nay, a vile one too?   275

ALTAMONT.

 Thou canst not, dar'st not mean it; speak again,
 Say, who is vile? But dare not name Calista.

HORATIO.

 I had not spoke at first unless compelled,
 And forced to clear myself; but since thus urged,
 I must avow I do not know a viler.   280

ALTAMONT.

 Thou wert my father's friend, he loved thee well;

A kind of venerable mark of him
Hangs round thee, and protects thee from my vengeance;
I cannot, dare not lift my sword against thee,
But henceforth never let me see thee more.   *Going out.* 285

HORATIO.

I love thee still, ungrateful as thou art,
And must and will preserve thee from dishonor,
Ev'n in despite of thee.   *Holds him.*

ALTAMONT.   Let go my arm.

HORATIO.

If honor be thy care, if thou wouldst live
Without the name of credulous, wittol husband,   290
Avoid thy bride, shun her detested bed;
The joys it yields are dashed with poison—

ALTAMONT.   Off!

To urge me but a minute more is fatal.

HORATIO.

She is polluted! Stained!

ALTAMONT.   Madness and raving!
But hence!

HORATIO.   Dishonored by the man you hate—   295

ALTAMONT.

I prithee loose me yet, for thy own sake,
If life be worth the keeping—

HORATIO.   By Lothario.

ALTAMONT.

Perdition take thee, villain, for the falsehood.   *Strikes him.*
Now nothing but thy life can make atonement.

HORATIO.

A blow! Thou hast used well—   *Draws.*

ALTAMONT.   This to thy heart—   300

HORATIO.

Yet hold! —By heav'n, his father's in his face.
Spite of my wrongs, my heart runs o'er with tenderness,
And I could rather die myself than hurt him.

ALTAMONT.

Defend thyself, for by my much wronged love,

300. hast used well] *Q, D1*; hast
used me well *D2–3*.

I swear the poor evasion shall not save thee.   305

HORATIO.

Yet hold! Thou know'st I dare! —Think how we've lived—

They fight: Altamont *presses on* Horatio, *who retires.*

Nay! Then 'tis brutal violence! And thus,
Thus nature bids me guard the life she gave.   *They fight.*

Lavinia *enters, and runs between their swords.*

LAVINIA.

My brother! My Horatio! Is it possible?
O, turn your cruel swords upon Lavinia!   310
If you must quench your impious rage in blood,
Behold, my heart shall give you all her store
To save those dearer streams that flow from yours.

ALTAMONT.

'Tis well thou hast found a safeguard; none but this,
No pow'r on earth could save thee from my fury.   315

LAVINIA.

O fatal, deadly sound!

HORATIO.   Safety from thee!
Away, vain boy! Hast thou forgot the reverence
Due to my arm, thy first, thy great example,
Which pointed out thy way to noble daring,
And showed thee what it was to be a man?   320

LAVINIA.

What busy, meddling fiend, what foe to goodness,
Could kindle such a discord? O, lay by
Those most ungentle looks and angry weapons.
Unless you mean my griefs and killing fears
Should stretch me out at your relentless feet,   325
A wretched corse, the victim of your fury.

HORATIO.

Ask'st thou what made us foes? 'Twas base ingratitude;
'Twas such a sin to friendship as heaven's mercy,
That strives with man's untoward, monstrous wickedness,
Unwearied with forgiving, scarce could pardon.   330
He who was all to me, child, brother, friend!

321. fiend] Q, D3; friend D1–2.

With barb'rous, bloody malice sought my life.

ALTAMONT.

Thou art my sister, and I would not make thee
The lonely mourner of a widowed bed;
Therefore thy husband's life is safe; but warn him   335
No more to know this hospitable roof.
He has but ill repaid Sciolto's bounty;
We must not meet; 'tis dangerous. Farewell.

He is going; Lavinia *holds him.*

LAVINIA.

Stay, Altamont, my brother, stay, if ever
Nature or what is nearer much than nature,   340
The kind consent of our agreeing minds,
Have made us dear to one another, stay,
And speak one gentle word to your Horatio.
Behold, his anger melts, he longs to love you,
To call you friend, then press you hard, with all   345
The tender, speechless joy of reconcilement.

ALTAMONT.

It cannot, sha' not be! You must not hold me.

LAVINIA.

Look kindly then!

ALTAMONT.   Each minute that I stay
Is a new injury to fair Calista.
From thy false friendship to her arms I'll fly;   350
There if in any pause of love I rest,
Breathless with bliss, upon her panting breast,
In broken, melting accents I will swear
Henceforth to trust my heart with none but her;
Then own the joys which on her charms attend   355
Have more than paid me for my faithless friend.

Altamont *breaks from* Lavinia, *and exit.*

HORATIO.

O, raise thee, my Lavinia, from the earth;
It is too much, this tide of flowing grief,
This wond'rous waste of tears, too much to give
To an ungrateful friend and cruel brother.   360

346. reconcilement] *Q, D1–2*; re-
concilements *D3.*

LAVINIA.

    Is there not cause for weeping? O, Horatio!
    A brother and a husband were my treasure;
    'Twas all the little wealth that poor Lavinia
    Saved from the shipwreck of her father's fortunes.
    One half is lost already; if thou leav'st me,   365
    If thou shouldst prove unkind to me as Altamont,
    Whom shall I find to pity my distress,
    To have compassion on a helpless wanderer,
    And give her where to lay her wretched head?

HORATIO.

    Why dost thou wound me with thy soft complainings?   370
    Though Altamont be false and use me hardly,
    Yet think not I impute his crimes to thee.
    Talk not of being forsaken, for I'll keep thee
    Next to my heart, my certain pledge of happiness.
    Heav'n formed thee gentle, fair, and full of goodness,   375
    And made thee all my portion here on earth;
    It gave thee to me as a large amends
    For fortune, friends, and all the world beside.

LAVINIA.

    Then you will love me still, cherish me ever,
    And hide me from misfortune in your bosom: 380
    Here end my cares, nor will I lose one thought
    How we shall live or purchase food or raiment.
    The holy pow'r, who clothes the senseless earth
    With woods, with fruits, with flow'rs and verdant grass,
    Whose bounteous hand feeds the whole brute creation,   385
    Knows all our wants and has enough to give us.

HORATIO.

    From Genoa, from falsehood and inconstancy,
    To some more honest, distant clime we'll go;
    Nor will I be beholding to my country
    For aught but thee, the partner of my flight.   390

LAVINIA.

    Yes, I will follow thee, forsake for thee
    My country, brother, friends, ev'n all I have;
    Though mine's a little all, yet were it more,
    And better far, it should be left for thee,
    And all that I would keep should be Horatio.   395

So when the merchant sees his vessel lost,
Though richly freighted from a foreign coast,
Gladly for life the treasure he would give,
And only wishes to escape and live.
Gold and his gains no more employ his mind,   400
But, driving o'er the billows with the wind,
Cleaves to one faithful plank and leaves the rest behind.

Exeunt.

End of the Third Act.

ACT IV

　　　　　　　　　SCENE, *a garden.*
　　　　　　　　　　Enter Altamont.

ALTAMONT.

　　With what unequal tempers are we formed?
　　One day the soul, supine with ease and fullness,
　　Revels secure, and fondly tells herself
　　The hour of evil can return no more;
　　The next, the spirits palled, and sick of riot,　　　　　　5
　　Turn all to discord, and we hate our beings,
　　Curse the past joy, and think it folly all,
　　And bitterness and anguish. O, last night!
　　What has ungrateful beauty paid me back
　　For all that mass of friendship which I squandered?　　10
　　Coldness, aversion, tears, and sullen sorrow
　　Dashed all my bliss, and damped my bridal bed.
　　Soon as the morning dawned, she vanished from me,
　　Relentless to the gentle call of love.
　　I have lost a friend, and I have gained—a wife!　　　15
　　Turn not to thought, my brain; but let me find
　　Some unfrequented shade; there lay me down,
　　And let forgetful dullness steal upon me
　　To soften and assuage this pain of thinking.　　　*Exit.*

　　　　　　　Enter Lothario *and* Calista.

LOTHARIO.

　　Weep not, my fair, but let the god of love　　　　　20
　　Laugh in thy eyes and revel in thy heart,
　　Kindle again his torch and hold it high
　　To light us to new joys; nor let a thought
　　Of discord or disquiet past, molest thee;
　　But to a long oblivion give thy cares,　　　　　　　25
　　And let us melt the present hour in bliss.

CALISTA.

　　Seek not to soothe me with thy false endearments,
　　To charm me with thy softness; 'tis in vain;

5. spirits] *D1–3*; spirit's *Q*.

Thou canst no more betray, nor I be ruined.
The hours of folly and of fond delight   30
Are wasted all and fled; those that remain
Are doomed to weeping, anguish, and repentance.
I come to charge thee with a long account
Of all the sorrows I have known already,
And all I have to come; thou hast undone me.   35

LOTHARIO.

Unjust Calista! Dost thou call it ruin
To love as we have done: to melt, to languish,
To wish for somewhat exquisitely happy,
And then be blest ev'n to that wish's height?
To die with joy, and straight to live again,   40
Speechless to gaze, and with tumultuous transport—

CALISTA.

O, let me hear no more; I cannot bear it,
'Tis deadly to remembrance; let that night,
That guilty night, be blotted from the year;
Let not the voice of mirth or music know it;   45
Let it be dark and desolate, no stars
To glitter o'er it; let it wish for light,
Yet want it still, and vainly wait the dawn;
For 'twas the night that gave me up to shame,
To sorrow, to perfidious, false Lothario.   50

LOTHARIO.

Hear this, ye pow'rs, mark how the fair deceiver
Sadly complains of violated truth;
She calls me false, ev'n she, the faithless she,
Whom day and night, whom heav'n and earth have heard
Sighing to vow, and tenderly protest   55
Ten thousand times, she would be only mine;
And yet, behold, she has giv'n herself away,
Fled from my arms, and wedded to another,
Ev'n to the man whom most I hate on earth—

CALISTA.

Art thou so base to upbraid me with a crime   60
Which nothing but thy cruelty could cause?
If indignation, raging in my soul
For thy unmanly insolence and scorn,
Urged me to do a deed of desperation,

And wound myself to be revenged on thee,   65
Think whom I should devote to death and hell,
Whom curse as my undoer but Lothario;
Hadst thou been just, not all Sciolto's pow'r,
Not all the vows and pray'rs of sighing Altamont
Could have prevailed, or won me to forsake thee.   70

LOTHARIO.

How have I failed in justice or in love?
Burns not my flame as brightly as at first?
Ev'n now my heart beats high, I languish for thee,
My transports are as fierce, as strong my wishes,
As if thou hadst never blest me with thy beauty.   75

CALISTA.

How didst thou dare to think that I would live
A slave to base desires and brutal pleasures,
To be a wretched wanton for thy leisure,
To toy and waste an hour of idle time with?
My soul disdains thee for so mean a thought.   80

LOTHARIO.

The driving storm of passion will have way,
And I must yield before it; wert thou calm,
Love, the poor criminal whom thou hast doomed,
Has yet a thousand tender things to plead
To charm thy rage and mitigate his fate.   85

Enter behind them Altamont.

ALTAMONT.

I have lost my peace— Ha! Do I live and wake!

CALISTA.

Hadst thou been true, how happy had I been!
Nor Altamont but thou hadst been my lord.
But wherefore named I happiness with thee?
It is for thee, for thee, that I am cursed;   90
For thee my secret soul each hour arraigns me,
Calls me to answer for my virtue stained,
My honor lost to thee; for thee it haunts me
With stern Sciolto vowing vengeance on me;
With Altamont complaining for his wrongs—   95

75. thy] *Q, D1–2*; my *D3*.

ALTAMONT.

    Behold him here—   *Coming forward.*

CALISTA.   Ah!—   *Starting.*

ALTAMONT.   The wretch, whom thou hast made!

    Curses and sorrows has thou heaped upon him,

    And vengeance is the only good is left.   *Drawing.*

LOTHARIO.

    Thou hast ta'en me somewhat unawares, 'tis true,

    But love and war take turns like day and night,   100

    And little preparation serves my turn,

    Equal to both, and armed for either field.

    We've long been foes; this moment ends our quarrel;

    Earth, heav'n, and fair Calista judge the combat.

CALISTA.

    Distraction! Fury! Sorrow! Shame, and death!   105

ALTAMONT.

    Thou hast talked too much; thy breath is poison to me;

    It taints the ambient air; this for thy father,

    This for Sciolto, and this last for Altamont.

They fight; Lothario *is wounded once or twice, and then falls.*

LOTHARIO.

    O, Altamont! Thy genius is the stronger;

    Thou hast prevailed! My fierce, ambitious soul,   110

    Declining, droops, and all her fires grow pale;

    Yet let not this advantage swell thy pride;

    I conquered in my turn; in love I triumphed;

    Those joys are lodged beyond the reach of fate;

    That sweet revenge comes smiling to my thoughts,   115

    Adorns my fall, and cheers my heart in dying.   *Dies.*

CALISTA.

    And what remains for me? Beset with shame,

    Encompassed round with wretchedness, there is

    But this one way to break the toil and 'scape.

She catches up Lothario's *sword, and offers to kill herself;* Altamont *runs to her, and wrests it from her.*

ALTAMONT.

    What means thy frantic rage?

CALISTA.   Off! Let me go.   120

ALTAMONT.

    O, thou hast more than murdered me, yet still,
    Still art thou here! And my soul starts with horror
    At thought of any danger that may reach thee.

CALISTA.

    Think'st thou I mean to live, to be forgiven?
    O, thou hast known but little of Calista;   125
    If thou hadst never heard my shame, if only
    The midnight moon and silent stars had seen it,
    I would not bear to be reproached by them,
    But dig down deep to find a grave beneath,
    And hide me from their beams.

SCIOLTO (*within*).   What ho, my son!   130

ALTAMONT.

    It is Sciolto calls; come near, and find me,
    The wretched'st thing of all my kind on earth.

CALISTA.

    Is it the voice of thunder, or my father?
    Madness! Confusion! Let the storm come on,
    Let the tumultuous roar drive all upon me,   135
    Dash my devoted bark; ye surges, break it;
    'Tis for my ruin that the tempest rises.
    When I am lost, sunk to the bottom low,
    Peace shall return, and all be calm again.

Enter Sciolto.

SCIOLTO.

    Ev'n now Rossano leaped the garden walls—   140
    Ha! Death has been among you—O my fears!
    Last night thou hadst a diff'rence with thy friend;
    The cause thou gav'st me for it was a damned one.
    Didst thou not wrong the man who told thee truth?
    Answer me quick—

ALTAMONT.   O, press me not to speak;   145
    Ev'n now my heart is breaking, and the mention
    Will lay me dead before you; see that body,
    And guess my shame, my ruin! O, Calista!

SCIOLTO.

    It is enough! But I am slow to execute,

And justice lingers in my lazy hand; 150
Thus let me wipe dishonor from my name,
And cut thee from the earth, thou stain to goodness.
                              Offers to kill Calista; Altamont *holds him.*

ALTAMONT.

Stay thee, Sciolto, thou rash father, stay,
Or turn the point on me, and through my breast
Cut out the bloody passage to Calista; 155
So shall my love be perfect, while for her
I die, for whom alone I wished to live.

CALISTA.

No, Altamont! My heart, that scorned thy love,
Shall never be indebted to thy pity;
Thus torn, defaced, and wretched as I seem, 160
Still I have something of Sciolto's virtue.
Yes, yes, my father, I applaud thy justice;
Strike home, and I will bless thee for the blow;
Be merciful, and free me from my pain;
'Tis sharp, 'tis terrible, and I could curse 165
The cheerful day, men, earth, and heav'n, and thee,
Ev'n thee, thou venerable good old man,
For being author of a wretch like me.

ALTAMONT.

Listen not to the wildness of her raving.
Remember nature! Should thy daughter's murder 170
Defile that hand so just, so great in arms,
Her blood would rest upon thee to posterity,
Pollute thy name, and sully all thy wars.

CALISTA.

Have I not wronged his gentle nature much?
And yet behold him pleading for my life. 175
Lost as thou art to virtue, O Calista,
I think thou canst not bear to be outdone;
Then haste to die, and be obliged no more.

SCIOLTO.

Thy pious care has giv'n me time to think,
And saved me from a crime; then rest, my sword; 180
To honor have I kept thee ever sacred,
Nor will I stain thee with a rash revenge;
But mark me well, I will have justice done;

Hope not to bear away thy crimes unpunished;
I will see justice executed on thee,   185
Ev'n to a Roman strictness; and thou, nature,
Or whatso'er thou art that plead'st within me,
Be still, thy tender strugglings are in vain.

CALISTA.

Then am I doomed to live and bear your triumph?
To groan beneath your scorn and fierce upbraidings,   190
Daily to be reproached, and have my misery
At morn, at noon, and night told over to me,
Lest my remembrance might grow pitiful
And grant a moment's interval of peace;
Is this, is this the mercy of a father?   195
I only beg to die, and he denies me.

SCIOLTO.

Hence from my sight; thy father cannot bear thee;
Fly with thy infamy to some dark cell
Where on the confines of eternal night,
Mourning, misfortune, cares, and anguish dwell;   200
Where ugly shame hides her opprobrious head,
And death and hell detested rule maintain;
There howl out the remainder of thy life,
And wish thy name may be no more remembered.

CALISTA.

Yes, I will fly to some such dismal place,   205
And be more cursed than you can wish I were;
This fatal form that drew on my undoing,
Fasting and tears and hardship shall destroy;
Nor light nor food nor comfort will I know,
Nor aught that may continue hated life.   210
Then when you see me meager, wan, and changed,
Stretched at my length, and dying in my cave,
On that cold earth I mean shall be my grave,
Perhaps you may relent and, sighing, say,
At length her tears have washed her stains away,   215
At length 'tis time her punishment should cease;
Die, thou poor suff'ring wretch, and be at peace.

Exit Calista.

SCIOLTO.

Who of my servants wait there?

-53-

Enter two or three servants.

On your lives
Take care my doors be guarded well, that none
Pass out or enter but by my appointment.   220

Exeunt servants.

ALTAMONT.

There is a fatal fury in your visage;
It blazes fierce, and menaces destruction;
My father, I am sick of many sorrows;
Ev'n now my easy heart is breaking with 'em;
Yet, above all, one fear distracts me most: 225
I tremble at the vengeance which you meditate
On the poor, faithless, lovely, dear Calista.

SCIOLTO.

Hast thou not read what brave Virginius did?
With his own hand he slew his only daughter
To save her from the fierce Decemvir's lust.   230
He slew her yet unspotted to prevent
The shame which she might know. Then what should I do?
But thou hast tied my hand—I wo' not kill her;
Yet by the ruin she has brought upon us,
The common infamy that brands us both,   235
She sha' not 'scape.

ALTAMONT.   You mean that she shall die then.

SCIOLTO.

Ask me not what, nor how, I have resolved,
For all within is anarchy and uproar.
O, Altamont! What a vast scheme of joy
Has this one day destroyed! Well did I hope   240
This daughter would have blessed my latter days,
That I should live to see you the world's wonder,
So happy, great, and good that none were like you,
While I, from busy life and care set free,
Had spent the evening of my age at home,   245

236. she shall die then.] *Q, D1–2;*
he shall die then? *D3.*

228–232. *Hast . . . know.*] According to Roman legend, the centurion
Virginius killed his daughter Virginia as the only means of securing her
honor against the attempts of the decemvir Appius Claudius.

Among a little prattling race of yours;
There, like an old man, talked a while, and then
Lain down and slept in peace. Instead of this,
Sorrow and shame must bring me to my grave;
O, damn her, damn her!

Enter a Servant.

SERVANT.   Arm yourself, my lord;   250
    Rossano, who but now escaped the garden,
    Has gathered in the street a band of rioters
    Who threaten you and all your friends with ruin
    Unless Lothario be returned in safety.

SCIOLTO.
    By heav'n, their fury rises to my wish,   255
    Nor shall misfortune know my house alone,
    But thou, Lothario, and thy race shall pay me
    For all the sorrows which my age is cursed with.
    I think my name as great, my friends as potent
    As any in the state; all shall be summoned;   260
    I know that all will join their hands to ours,
    And vindicate thy vengeance. Raise the body,
    And bear it in; his friends shall buy him dearly;
    I will have blood for ransom; when our force
    Is full and armed, we shall expect thy sword   265
    To join with us and sacrifice to justice.   *Exit* Sciolto.

    The body of Lothario *is carried off by servants.*   *Manet* Altamont.

ALTAMONT.
    There is a stupid weight upon my senses,
    A dismal, sullen stillness that succeeds
    The storm of rage and grief, like silent death
    After the tumult and the noise of life.   270
    Would it were death, as sure 'tis wond'rous like it,
    For I am sick of living, my soul's palled;
    She kindles not with anger or revenge;
    Love was th'informing, active fire within;
    Now that is quenched, the mass forgets to move,   275
    And longs to mingle with its kindred earth.

    A tumultuous noise with clashing of swords, as at a little distance.

Enter Lavinia *with two servants, their swords drawn.*

LAVINIA.

Fly, swiftly fly to my Horatio's aid,
Nor lose you vain, officious cares on me;
Bring me my lord, my husband to my arms;
He is Lavinia's life; bring him me safe,   280
And I shall be at ease, be well and happy.   *Exeunt servants.*

ALTAMONT.

Art thou Lavinia? O, what barb'rous hand
Could wring thy poor, defenseless innocence
And leave such marks of more than savage fury?

LAVINIA.

My brother! O, my heart is full of fears;   285
Perhaps ev'n now my dear Horatio bleeds.
Not far from hence, as passing to the port,
By a mad multitude we were surrounded,
Who ran upon us with uplifted swords
And cried aloud for vengeance and Lothario.   290
My lord with ready boldness stood the shock
To shelter me from danger, but in vain,
Had not a party from Sciolto's palace
Rushed out and snatched me from amidst the fray.

ALTAMONT.

What of my friend?

LAVINIA (*looking out*).   Ha! By my joys, 'tis he;   295
He lives, he comes to bless me, he is safe!

Enter Horatio *with two or three* Servants, *their swords drawn.*

FIRST SERVANT.

'Twere at the utmost hazard of your life
To venture forth again till we are stronger;
Their number trebles ours.

HORATIO.   No matter, let it;
Death is not half so shocking as that traitor.   300
My honest soul is mad with indignation
To think her plainness could be so abused
As to mistake that wretch and call him friend;

278. you] *Q*; your *D1–3.*

---

287. *port*] portal, gate.

I cannot bear the sight.

ALTAMONT.   Open, thou earth,
 Gape wide, and take me down to thy dark bosom   305
 To hide me from Horatio.

HORATIO.   O, Lavinia,
 Believe not but I joy to see thee safe.
 Would our ill fortune had not drove us hither;
 I could ev'n wish we rather had been wrecked
 On any other shore than saved on this.   310

LAVINIA.
 O, let us bless the mercy that preserved us,
 That gracious pow'r that saved us for each other,
 And, to adorn the sacrifice of praise,
 Offer forgiveness too; be thou like heav'n,
 And put away th'offenses of thy friend   315
 Far, far from thy remembrance.

ALTAMONT.   I have marked him
 To see if one forgiving glance stole hither,
 If any spark of friendship were alive
 That would by sympathy at meeting glow,
 And strive to kindle up the flame anew;   320
 'Tis lost, 'tis gone, his soul is quite estranged,
 And knows me for its counterpart no more.

HORATIO.
 Thou know'st thy rule, thy empire in Horatio,
 Nor canst thou ask in vain, command in vain
 Where nature, reason, nay, where love is judge;   325
 But when you urge my temper to comply
 With what it most abhors, I cannot do it.

LAVINIA.
 Where didst thou get this sullen, gloomy hate?
 It was not in thy nature to be thus;
 Come, put if off, and let thy heart be cheerful,   330
 Be gay again, and know the joys of friendship,
 The trust, security, and mutual tenderness,
 The double joys, where each is glad for both;
 Friendship, the wealth, the last retreat and strength,
 Secure against ill fortune and the world.   335

HORATIO.
 I am not apt to take a light offense,

But patient of the failings of my friends,
And willing to forgive; but when an injury
Stabs to the heart and rouses my resentment
(Perhaps it is the fault of my rude nature),   340
I own I cannot easily forget it.

ALTAMONT.

Thou hast forgot me.

HORATIO.   No.

ALTAMONT.   Why are thy eyes
Impatient of me then, scornful and fierce?

HORATIO.

Because they speak the meaning of my heart;
Because they are honest and disdain a villain.   345

ALTAMONT.

I have wronged thee much, Horatio.

HORATIO.   True, thou hast;
When I forget it, may I be a wretch
Vile as thyself, a false, perfidious fellow,
An infamous, believing, British husband.

ALTAMONT.

I've wronged thee much, and heav'n has well avenged it.   350
I have not, since we parted, been at peace,
Nor known one joy sincere; our broken friendship
Pursued me to the last retreat of love,
Stood glaring like a ghost, and made me cold with horror.
Misfortunes on misfortunes press upon me,   355
Swell o'er my head like waves, and dash me down.
Sorrow, remorse, and shame have torn my soul;
They hang like winter on my youthful hopes,
And blast the spring and promise of my year.

LAVINIA.

So flow'rs are gathered to adorn a grave,   360
To lose their freshness amongst bones and rottenness,
And have their odors stifled in the dust.
Canst thou hear this, thou cruel, hard Horatio?
Canst thou behold thy Altamont undone?
That gentle, that dear youth! Canst thou behold him,   365
His poor heart broken, death in his pale visage,

341. forget] *Q–D1*; forgive *D2–3*.

And groaning out his woes, yet stand unmoved?

HORATIO.
>   The brave and wise I pity in misfortune,
>   But when ingratitude and folly suffers,
>   'Tis weakness to be touched.

ALTAMONT.   I wo' not ask thee   370
>   To pity or forgive me, but confess
>   This scorn, this insolence of hate is just;
>   'Tis constancy of mind and manly in thee.
>   But, O, had I been wronged by thee, Horatio,
>   There is a yielding softness in my heart   375
>   Could ne'er have stood it out, but I had ran
>   With streaming eyes and open arms upon thee,
>   And pressed thee close, close!

HORATIO.   I must hear no more;
>   The weakness is contagious; I shall catch it,
>   And be a tame, fond wretch.

LAVINIA.   Where wouldst thou go?   380
>   Wouldst thou part thus? You sha' not, 'tis impossible;
>   For I will bar thy passage, kneeling thus;
>   Perhaps thy cruel hand may spurn me off,
>   But I will throw my body in thy way,
>   And thou shalt trample o'er my faithful bosom,   385
>   Tread on me, wound me, kill me ere thou pass.

ALTAMONT.
>   Urge not in vain thy pious suit, Lavinia;
>   I have enough to rid me of my pain.
>   Calista, thou hadst reached my heart before;
>   To make all sure, my friend repeats the blow.   390
>   But in the grave our cares shall be forgotten;
>   There love and friendship cease.   *Falls.*

Lavinia *runs to him, and endeavors to raise him.*

LAVINIA.   Speak to me, Altamont.
>   He faints! He dies! Now turn and see thy triumph,
>   My brother! But our cares shall end together;
>   Here will I lay me down by thy dear side,   395
>   Bemoan thy too hard fate, then share it with thee,
>   And never see my cruel lord again.

Horatio *runs to* Altamont, *and raises him in his arms.*

HORATIO.

> It is too much to bear! Look up, my Altamont!
> My stubborn, unrelenting heart has killed him.
> Look up and bless me, tell me that thou liv'st. 400
> O, I have urged they gentleness too far; *He revives.*
> Do thou and my Lavinia both forgive me;
> A flood of tenderness comes o'er my soul;
> I cannot speak! I love, forgive, and pity thee!

ALTAMONT.

> I thought that nothing could have stayed my soul, 405
> That long ere this her flight had reached the stars;
> But thy known voice has lured her back again.
> Methinks I fain would set all right with thee,
> Make up this most unlucky breach, and then,
> With thine and heav'n's forgiveness on my soul, 410
> Shrink to my grave, and be at ease forever.

HORATIO.

> By heav'n, my heart bleeds for thee; ev'n this moment
> I feel thy pangs of disappointed love.
> Is it not pity that this youth should fail,
> That all this wond'rous goodness should be lost, 415
> And the world never know it? O, my Altamont!
> Give me thy sorrows, let me bear 'em for thee,
> And shelter thee from ruin.

LAVINIA. O, my brother!

> Think not but we will share in all thy woes;
> We'll sit all day and tell sad tales of love, 420
> And when we light upon some faithless woman,
> Some beauty, like Calista, false and fair,
> We'll fix our grief and our complaining there;
> We'll curse the nymph that drew the ruin on,
> And mourn the youth that was like thee undone. *Exeunt.* 425

End of the Fourth Act.

ACT V

SCENE *is a room hung with black: on one side, Lothario's body on a bier;*
on the other, a table with a skull and other bones, a book, and a lamp on it.
Calista is discovered on a couch in black, her hair hanging loose and dis-
ordered; after music and a song, she rises and comes forward.

SONG

I

Hear, you midnight phantoms, hear,　⎫
You who pale and wan appear,　　　　⎬
And fill the wretch, who wakes, with fear.⎭
You who wander, scream, and groan,
Round the mansions once your own,　　　　　　5
You whom still your crimes upbraid,
You who rest not with the dead;
From the coverts where you stray,
Where you lurk and shun the day,
From the charnel and the tomb,　　　　　　　10
Hither haste ye, hither come.

II

Chide Calista for delay,　　　⎫
Tell her 'tis for her you stay;　⎬
Bid her die and come away. ⎭
See the sexton with his spade,　　　　　　　15
See the grave already made;
Listen, fair one, to thy knell,
This music is thy passing bell.

CALISTA.

'Tis well! These solemn sounds, this pomp of horror
Are fit to feed the frenzy in my soul;　　　　　20
Here's room for meditation, ev'n to madness,
Till the mind burst with thinking; this dull flame
Sleeps in the socket; sure the book was left
To tell me something—for inspiration then—
He teaches holy sorrow and contrition　　　　25
And penitence— Is it become an art then?

A trick that lazy, dull, luxurious gown-men
Can teach us to do over? I'll no more on't;

         Throwing away the book.

I have more real anguish in my heart
Than all their pedant discipline e'er knew.   30
What charnel has been rifled for these bones?
Fie! This is pageantry—they look uncouthly,
But what of that? If he or she that owned 'em
Safe from disquiet sit, and smile to see
The farce their miserable relics play.   35
But here's a sight is terrible indeed;
Is this that haughty, gallant, gay Lothario?
That dear perfidious— Ah! how pale he looks!
How grim with clotted blood and those dead eyes!
Ascend, ye ghosts, fantastic forms of night,   40
In all your diff'rent, dreadful shapes ascend,
And match the present horror if you can.

      Enter Sciolto.

SCIOLTO.

This dead of night, this silent hour of darkness
Nature for rest ordained and soft repose,
And yet distraction and tumultuous jars   45
Keep all our frighted citizens awake;
The senate, weak, divided, and irresolute,
Want pow'r to succor the afflicted state.
Vainly in words and long debates they're wise,
While the fierce factions scorn their peaceful orders, 50
And drown the voice of law in noise and anarchy.
Amidst the general wreck, see where she stands,

         Pointing to Calista.

Like Helen in the night when Troy was sacked,
Spectatress of the mischief which she made.

CALISTA.

It is Sciolto! Be thyself, my soul;   55
Be strong to bear his fatal indignation,

---

27. *gown-men*] scholars.
53–54. *Like . . . made.*] See Virgil, *Aeneid*, II, ll. 567–574.

That he may see thou art not lost so far
But somewhat still of his great spirit lives
In the forlorn Calista.

SCIOLTO.   Thou wert once
My daughter.

CALISTA.   Happy were it I had died,   60
And never lost that name.

SCIOLTO.   That's something yet;
Thou wert the very darling of my age;
I thought the day too short to gaze upon thee,
That all the blessings I could gather for thee
By cares on earth and by my pray'rs to heav'n   65
Were little for my fondness to bestow;
Why didst thou turn to folly, then, and curse me?

CALISTA.
Because my soul was rudely drawn from yours,
A poor, imperfect copy of my father,
Where goodness and the strength of manly virtue   70
Was thinly planted, and the idle void
Filled up with light belief and easy fondness;
It was because I loved, and was a woman.

SCIOLTO.
Hadst thou been honest, thou hadst been a cherubin;
But of that joy, as of a gem long lost,   75
Beyond redemption gone, think we no more.
Hast thou e'er dared to meditate on death?

CALISTA.
I have, as on the end of shame and sorrow.

SCIOLTO.
Ha! Answer me! Say, has thou coolly thought?
'Tis not the stoic's lessons got by rote,   80
The pomp of words, and pedant dissertations
That can sustain thee in that hour of terror;
Books have taught cowards to talk nobly of it,
But when the trial comes, they start and stand aghast.
Hast thou considered what may happen after it?   85
How thy account may stand, and what to answer?

CALISTA.
I have turned my eyes inward upon myself,
Where foul offense and shame have laid all waste;

Therefore my soul abhors the wretched dwelling,
And longs to find some better place of rest.   90

SCIOLTO.

    'Tis justly thought, and worthy of that spirit
That dwelt in ancient Latian breasts when Rome
Was mistress of the world. I would go on
And tell thee all my purpose, but it sticks
Here at my heart, and cannot find a way.   95

CALISTA.

    Then spare the telling, if it be a pain,
And write the meaning with your poniard here.

SCIOLTO.

    O, truly guessed—seest thou this trembling hand—

Holding up a dagger.

Thrice justice urged—and thrice the slack'ning sinews
Forgot their office and confessed the father;   100
At length the stubborn virtue has prevailed;
It must, it must be so— O, take it then,   *Giving the dagger.*
And know the rest untaught.

CALISTA.   I understand you;
It is but thus, and both are satisfied.

She offers to kill herself; Sciolto *catches hold of her arm.*

SCIOLTO.

    A moment, give me yet a moment's space;   105
The stern, the rigid judge has been obeyed;
Now nature and the father claim their turns;
I have held the balance with an iron hand,
And put off ev'ry tender, human thought,
To doom my child to death; but spare my eyes   110
The most unnatural sight, lest their strings crack,
And my old brain split and grow mad with horror.

CALISTA.

    Ha! Is is possible? And is there yet
Some little, dear remain of love and tenderness
For poor, undone Calista in your heart?   115

SCIOLTO.

    O, when I think what pleasure I took in thee,

95. Here] *D1–3*; Hear *Q.*

What joys thou gav'st me in thy prattling infancy,
Thy sprightly wit and early blooming beauty,
How I have stood and fed my eyes upon thee,
Then lifted up my hands and, wond'ring, blessed thee;   120
By my strong grief, my heart ev'n melts within me;
I could curse nature and that tyrant, honor,
For making me thy father and thy judge;
Thou art my daughter still.

CALISTA.   For that kind word
Thus let me fall, thus humbly to the earth,   125
Weep on your feet, and bless you for this goodness;
O, 'tis too much for this offending wretch,
This parricide, that murders with her crimes,
Shortens her father's age, and cuts him off
Ere little more than half his years be numbered.   130

SCIOLTO.
Would it were otherwise! But thou must die—

CALISTA.
That I must die, it is my only comfort;
Death is the privilege of human nature,
And life without it were not worth our taking;
Thither the poor, the pris'ner, and the mourner   135
Fly for relief and lay their burdens down.
Come then, and take me now to thy cold arms,
Thou meager shade; here let me breathe my last,
Charmed with my father's pity and forgiveness
More than if angels tuned their golden viols,   140
And sung a requiem to my parting soul.

SCIOLTO.
I am summoned hence; ere this my friends expect me;
There is I know not what of sad presage
That tells me I shall never see thee more;
If it be so, this is our last farewell,   145
And these the parting pangs which nature feels
When anguish rends the heartstrings—O, my daughter!
                                        Exit Sciolto.

CALISTA.
Now think thou, cursed Calista, now behold
The desolation, horror, blood, and ruin
Thy crimes and fatal folly spread around   150

That loudly cry for vengeance on thy head;
Yet heav'n, who knows our weak, imperfect natures,
How blind with passions and how prone to evil,
Makes not too strict enquiry for offenses,
But is atoned by penitence and pray'r.   155
Cheap recompense! Here 'twould not be received;
Nothing but blood can make the expiation,
And cleanse the soul from inbred, deep pollution.
And see, another injured wretch is come
To call for justice from my tardy hand.   160

Enter Altamont.

ALTAMONT.

Hail to you horrors! Hail, thou house of death!
And thou, the lovely mistress of these shades,
Whose beauty gilds the more than midnight darkness,
And makes it grateful as the dawn of day.
O, take me in, a fellow-mourner with thee;   165
I'll number groan for groan and tear for tear;
And when the fountains of thy eyes are dry,
Mine shall supply the stream and weep for both.

CALISTA.

I know thee well; thou art the injured Altamont;
Thou com'st to urge me with the wrongs I ha' done thee;   170
But know I stand upon the brink of life,
And in a moment mean to set me free
From shame and thy upbraiding.

ALTAMONT.   Falsely, falsely

Dost thou accuse me. When did I complain
Or murmur at my fate? For thee I have   175
Forgot the temper of Italian husbands,
And fondness has prevailed upon revenge;
I bore my load of infamy with patience,
As holy men do punishments from heav'n,
Nor thought it hard, because it came from thee;   180
O, then forbid me not to mourn thy loss,
To wish some better fate had ruled our loves,
And that Calista had been mine, and true.

167. fountains] *JRS*; fountain *Q*,
D1–3.

CALISTA.
O, Altamont, 'tis hard for souls like mine,
Haughty and fierce, to yield they have done amiss;   185
But, O, behold my proud, disdainful heart
Bends to thy gentler virtue; yes, I own,
Such is thy truth, thy tenderness and love,
Such are the graces that adorn thy youth,
That were I not abandoned to destruction,   190
With thee I might have lived for ages blest,
And died in peace within thy faithful arms.

ALTAMONT.
Then happiness is still within our reach;
Here let remembrance lose our past misfortunes,
Tear all records that hold the fatal story;   195
Here let our joys begin, from hence go on
In long successive order.

CALISTA.   What! In death?

ALTAMONT.
Then art thou fixed to die? But be it so,
We'll go together; my advent'rous love
Shall follow thee to those uncertain beings;   200
Whether our lifeless shades are doomed to wander
In gloomy groves with discontented ghosts,
Or whether through the upper air we fleet,
And tread the fields of light, still I'll pursue thee
Till fate ordains that we shall part no more.   205

CALISTA.
O, no! Heav'n has some better lot in store
To crown thee with; live and be happy long;
Live for some maid that shall deserve thy goodness,
Some kind, unpracticed heart that never yet
Has listened to the false ones of thy sex,   210
Nor known the arts of ours; she shall reward thee,
Meet thee with virtues equal to thy own,
Charm thee with sweetness, beauty, and with truth,
Be blest in thee alone, and thou in her.

Enter Horatio.

HORATIO.
Now mourn indeed, ye miserable pair,   215

For now the measure of your woes is full.

ALTAMONT.

What dost thou mean, Horatio?

HORATIO.   O, 'tis dreadful;

The great, the good Sciolto dies this moment.

CALISTA.

My father!

ALTAMONT.   That's a deadly stroke indeed.

HORATIO.

220

> Not long ago he privately went forth,
> Attended but by few, and those unbidden;
> I heard which way he took, and straight pursued him,
> But found him compassed by Lothario's faction,
> Almost alone amidst a crowd of foes;
> Too late we brought him aid and drove them back;   225
> Ere that his frantic valor had provoked
> The death he seemed to wish for from their swords.

CALISTA.

> And dost thou bear me yet, thou patient earth?
> Dost thou not labor with my murd'rous weight?
> And you, ye glitt'ring, heav'nly host of stars,   230
> Hide your fair heads in clouds, or I shall blast you,
> For I am all contagion, death, and ruin,
> And nature sickens at me; rest, thou world,
> This parricide shall be thy plague no more;
> Thus, thus I set thee free.   *Stabs herself.*

HORATIO.   O fatal rashness!   235

ALTAMONT.

> Thou dost instruct me well; to length life
> Is but to trifle now.

Altamont *offers to kill himself*; Horatio *prevents him, and wrests his sword from him.*

HORATIO.   Ha! What means

> The frantic Altamont? Some foe to man
> Has breathed on ev'ry breast contagious fury
> And epidemic madness.

Enter Sciolto, *pale and bloody, supported by servants.*

CALISTA.   O my heart!   240

Well may'st thou fail, for see, the spring that fed
Thy vital stream is wasted and runs low.
My father! Will you now at last forgive me,
If after all my crimes and all your sufferings
I call you once again by that dear name?   245
Will you forget my shame and those wide wounds,
Lift up your hand, and bless me ere I go
Down to my dark abode?

SCIOLTO.   Alas, my daughter!
Thou hast rashly ventured in a stormy sea,
Where life, fame, virtue, all were wrecked and lost;   250
But sure thou hast borne thy part in all the anguish,
And smarted with the pain; then rest in peace;
Let silence and oblivion hide thy name,
And save thee from the malice of posterity;
And may'st thou find with heav'n the same forgiveness   255
As with thy father here. Die, and be happy.

CALISTA.
Celestial sounds! Peace dawns upon my soul,
And ev'ry pain grows less. —O gentle Altamont,
Think not too hardly of me when I'm gone,
But pity me. Had I but early known   260
Thy wond'rous worth, thou excellent young man,
We had been happier both. Now 'tis too late,
And yet my eyes take pleasure to behold thee;
Thou wert their last dear object. —Mercy, heav'n!   *She dies.*

ALTAMONT.
Cold! Dead and cold! And yet thou art not changed,   265
But lovely still! Hadst thou a thousand faults,
What heart so hard, what virtue so severe
But at that beauty must of force relented,
Melted to pity, love, and to forgiveness?

SCIOLTO.
O, turn thee from the fatal object; Altamont,   270
Come near, and let me bless thee ere I die.
To thee and brave Horatio I bequeath
My fortunes. Lay me by thy noble father,
And love my memory as thou hast done his,

270. the] *Q, D1*; that *D2–3*.

For thou hast been my son. —O gracious heav'n!   275
Thou that hast endless blessings still in store
For virtue and for filial piety,
Let grief, disgrace, and want be far away,
But multiply thy mercies on his head;
Let honor, greatness, goodness still be with him,   280
And peace in all his ways.   *He dies.*
ALTAMONT.   Take, take it all;
To thee, Horatio, I resign the gift
While I pursue my father and my love
And find my only portion in the grave.   [*He faints.*]
HORATIO.
The storm of grief bears hard upon his youth,   285
And bends him like a drooping flower to earth.
Raise him, and bear him in.   Altamont *is carried off.*
By such examples are we taught to prove
The sorrows that attend unlawful love;
Death or some worse misfortunes soon divide   290
The injured bridegroom from his guilty bride;
If you would have the nuptial union last,
Let virtue be the bond that ties it fast.   *Exeunt omnes.*

The End of the Fifth Act.

284. S.D.] *MJ; omit. Q, D1–3.*

EPILOGUE

Spoken by Mrs. Bracegirdle, who played Lavinia

You see the tripping dame could find no favor;
Dearly she paid for breach of good behavior,
Nor could her loving husband's fondness save her.
Italian ladies lead but scurvy lives;
There's dreadful dealing with eloping wives;   5
Thus 'tis because these husbands are obeyed
By force of laws which for themselves they made.
With tales of old prescriptions they confine
The right of marriage-rule to their male line,
And huff and domineer by right divine.   10
Had we the pow'r, we'd make the tyrants know
What 'tis to fail in duties which they owe;
We'd teach the saunt'ring squire who loves to roam,
Forgetful of his own dear spouse and home,
Who snores at night supinely by her side,   15
'Twas not for this the nuptial knot was tied.
The plodding pettifogger and the cit
Have learned at least this modern way of wit:
Each ill-bred, senseless rogue, though ne'er so dull,
Has th'impudence to think his wife a fool;   20
He spends the night where merry wags resort,
With joking clubs and eighteen-penny port,
While she, poor soul, 's contented to regale
By a sad sea-coal fire with wigs and ale.
Well may the cuckold-making tribe find grace,   25
And fill an absent husband's empty place;
If you would e'er bring constancy in fashion,
You men must first begin the reformation.
Then shall the golden age of love return,
No turtle for her wand'ring mate shall mourn,   30
No foreign charms shall cause domestic strife,

---

17. *cit*] the familiar abbreviated form of "citizen," referring to a resident of the City of London.

24. *wigs*] small cakes made with fine flour.

30. *turtle*] turtle dove.

But ev'ry married man shall toast his wife;
Phyllis shall not be to the country sent,
For carnivals in town to keep a tedious Lent;
Lampoons shall cease, and envious scandal die,   35
And all shall live in peace, like my good man and I.

Appendix

Chronology

Approximate dates on indicated by *. Dates for plays are those on which they were first made public, either on stage or in print.

Political and Literary Events	*Life and Principal Works of Rowe*

1631
Death of Donne.
John Dryden born.

1633
Samuel Pepys born.

1635
Sir George Etherege born.*

1640
Aphra Behn born.*

1641
William Wycherley born.*

1642
First Civil War began (ended 1646).
Theaters closed by Parliament.
Thomas Shadwell born.*

1648
Second Civil War.
Nathaniel Lee born.*

1649
Execution of Charles I.

1650
Jeremy Collier born.

1651
Hobbes' *Leviathan* published.

1652
First Dutch War began (ended 1654).
Thomas Otway born.

1656

D'Avenant's *THE SIEGE OF RHODES* performed at Rutland House.

1657

John Dennis born.

1658

Death of Oliver Cromwell.

D'Avenant's *THE CRUELTY OF THE SPANIARDS IN PERU* performed at the Cockpit.

1660

Restoration of Charles II.

Theatrical patents granted to Thomas Killigrew and Sir William D'Avenant, authorizing them to form, respectively, the King's and the Duke of York's Companies.

Pepys began his diary.

1661

Cowley's *THE CUTTER OF COLEMAN STREET*.

D'Avenant's *THE SIEGE OF RHODES* (expanded to two parts).

1662

Charter granted to the Royal Society.

1663

Dryden's *THE WILD GALLANT*.

Tuke's *THE ADVENTURES OF FIVE HOURS*.

1664

Sir John Vanbrugh born.

Dryden's *THE RIVAL LADIES*.

Dryden and Howard's *THE INDIAN QUEEN*.

Etherege's *THE COMICAL REVENGE*.

1665

Second Dutch War began (ended 1667).

Great Plague.

Dryden's *THE INDIAN EM-PEROR.*

Orrery's *MUSTAPHA.*

1666

Fire of London.

Death of James Shirley.

1667

Jonathan Swift born.

Milton's *Paradise Lost* published.

Sprat's *The History of the Royal Society* published.

Dryden's *SECRET LOVE.*

1668

Death of D'Avenant.

Dryden made Poet Laureate.

Dryden's *An Essay of Dramatic Poesy* published.

Shadwell's *THE SULLEN LOVERS.*

1669

Pepys terminated his diary.

Susannah Centlivre born.

1670

William Congreve born.

Dryden's *THE CONQUEST OF GRANADA*, Part I.

1671

Dorset Garden Theatre (Duke's Company) opened.

Colley Cibber born.

Milton's *Paradise Regained* and *Samson Agonistes* published.

Dryden's *THE CONQUEST OF GRANADA*, Part II.

THE REHEARSAL, by the Duke of Buckingham and others.

Wycherley's *LOVE IN A WOOD.*

1672

Third Dutch War began (ended 1674).

Joseph Addison born.

Richard Steele born.

Dryden's *MARRIAGE A LA MODE.*

1674

New Drury Lane Theatre (King's Company) opened.

Death of Milton.

Thomas Rymer's *Reflections on Aristotle's Treatise of Poesy* (translation of Rapin) published.

Born June 20, Little Barford, Bedfordshire.

1675

Dryden's *AURENG-ZEBE.*
Wycherley's *THE COUNTRY WIFE.* *

1676

Etherege's *THE MAN OF MODE.*
Otway's *DON CARLOS.*
Shadwell's *THE VIRTUOSO.*
Wycherley's *THE PLAIN DEALER.*

1677

Aphra Behn's *THE ROVER.*
Dryden's *ALL FOR LOVE.*
Lee's *THE RIVAL QUEENS.*
Rymer's *Tragedies of the Last Age Considered* published.

1678

Popish Plot.

George Farquhar born.

Bunyan's *Pilgrim's Progress* (Part I) published.

1679

Exclusion Bill introduced.

Death of Thomas Hobbes.

Death of Roger Boyle, Earl of Orrery.

Charles Johnson born.

1680

Death of Samuel Butler.

Death of John Wilmot, Earl of Rochester.

Dryden's *THE SPANISH FRIAR.*
Lee's *LUCIUS JUNIUS BRUTUS.*
Otway's *THE ORPHAN.*

1681

Charles II dissolved Parliament at Oxford.

Dryden's *Absalom and Achitophel* published.

Tate's adaptation of *KING LEAR*.

1682

The King's and the Duke of York's Companies merged into the United Company.

Dryden's *The Medal, MacFlecknoe*, and *Religio Laici* published.

Otway's *VENICE PRESERVED*.

1683

Rye House Plot.

Death of Thomas Killigrew.

Crowne's *CITY POLITIQUES*.

1685

Death of Charles II; accession of James II.

Revocation of the Edict of Nantes.

The Duke of Monmouth's Rebellion.

Death of Otway.

John Gay born.

Crowne's *SIR COURTLY NICE*.

Dryden's *ALBION AND ALBANIUS*.

1687

Death of the Duke of Buckingham.

Dryden's *The Hind and the Panther* published.

Newton's *Principia* published.

1688

The Revolution.

Alexander Pope born.

Shadwell's *THE SQUIRE OF ALSATIA*.

1689

The War of the League of Augsburg began (ended 1697).

Toleration Act.

Death of Aphra Behn.

Shadwell made Poet Laureate.

Dryden's *DON SEBASTIAN*.

Shadwell's *BURY FAIR*.

1690

Battle of the Boyne.
Locke's *Two Treatises of Government*
and *An Essay Concerning Human
Understanding* published.

1691

Death of Etherege.*   Admitted to the Middle Temple.
Langbaine's *An Account of the
English Dramatic Poets* published.

1692

Death of Lee.
Death of Shadwell.
Tate made Poet Laureate.

1693

George Lillo born.*
Rymer's *A Short View of Tragedy*
published.
Congreve's *THE OLD BACHELOR.*

1694

Death of Queen Mary.
Southerne's *THE FATAL MAR-
RIAGE.*

1695

Group of actors led by Thomas
Betterton left Drury Lane and
established a new company at
Lincoln's Inn Fields.
Congreve's *LOVE FOR LOVE.*
Southerne's *OROONOKO.*

1696

Cibber's *LOVE'S LAST SHIFT.*   Called to the Bar.
Vanbrugh's *THE RELAPSE.*

1697

Treaty of Ryswick ended the War
of the League of Augsburg.
Charles Macklin born.
Congreve's *THE MOURNING
BRIDE.*
Vanbrugh's *THE PROVOKED
WIFE.*

1698

Collier controversy started with the   Married first wife, Antonia Parsons.

publication of *A Short View of the Immorality and Profaneness of the English Stage.*

1699

Farquhar's *THE CONSTANT COUPLE.*

Son, John, born.*

1700

Death of Dryden.

Blackmore's *Satire against Wit* published.

Congreve's *THE WAY OF THE WORLD.*

THE AMBITIOUS STEP-MOTHER opened at Lincoln's Inn Fields in December.*

1701

Act of Settlement.

War of the Spanish Succession began (ended 1713).

Death of James II.

Steele's *THE FUNERAL.*

TAMERLANE opened at Lincoln's Inn Fields in December.*

1702

Death of William III; accession of Anne.

The Daily Courant began publication.

Cibber's *SHE WOULD AND SHE WOULD NOT.*

1703

Death of Samuel Pepys.

THE FAIR PENITENT opened at Lincoln's Inn Fields in March.*

1704

Capture of Gibraltar; Battle of Blenheim.

Defoe's *The Review* began publication (1704–1713).

Swift's *A Tale of a Tub* and *The Battle of the Books* published.

Cibber's *THE CARELESS HUS-BAND.*

THE BITER opened at Lincoln's Inn Fields in November.*

1705.

Haymarket Theatre opened.

Steele's *THE TENDER HUS-BAND.*

ULYSSES opened at the Queen's Theatre in the Haymarket on November 23.

1706

Battle of Ramillies.

Death of first wife.

Farquhar's *THE RECRUITING OFFICER*.

1707

Union of Scotland and England.
Death of Farquhar.
Henry Fielding born.
Farquhar's *THE BEAUX' STRAT-AGEM*.

THE ROYAL CONVERT opened at the Queen's Theatre in the Haymarket on November 25.

1708

Downes' *Roscius Anglicanus* published.

John Ozell's translation of Boileau's *Lutrin* published, with commentary by Rowe.

1709

Samuel Johnson born.
The Tatler began publication (1709–1711).
Centlivre's *THE BUSY BODY*.

Appointed Secretary to the Duke of Queensberry.
Rowe's edition of Shakespeare published.

1711

Shaftesbury's *Characteristics* published.
The Spectator began publication (1711–1712).
Pope's *An Essay on Criticism* published.

1713

Treaty of Utrecht ended the War of the Spanish Succession.
Addison's *CATO*.

1714

Death of Anne; accession of George I.
Steele became Governor of Drury Lane.
John Rich assumed management of Lincoln's Inn Fields.
Centlivre's *THE WONDER: A WOMAN KEEPS A SECRET*.

THE TRAGEDY OF JANE SHORE opened at Drury Lane on February 2.
Poems on Several Occasions published.
Appointed Land Surveyor of the Customs by George I.

1715

Jacobite Rebellion.
Death of Tate.
Death of Wycherley.

THE TRAGEDY OF LADY JANE GRAY opened at Drury Lane on April 20.
Named Poet Laureate on August 1.

Married second wife, Anne Devenish.

Appointed Clerk of the Council of the Prince of Wales.

1716
Addison's *THE DRUMMER.*

1717
David Garrick born.
Cibber's *THE NON-JUROR.*
Gay, Pope, and Arbuthnot's *THREE HOURS AFTER MARRIAGE.*

1718
Centlivre's *A BOLD STROKE FOR A WIFE.*

Daughter, Charlotte, born.*
Died December 5; buried in Westminster Abbey.

1719
Death of Addison.
Defoe's *Robinson Crusoe* published.
Young's *BUSIRIS, KING OF EGYPT.*

Translation of Lucan's *Pharsalia* published.

1720
South Sea Bubble.
Samuel Foote born.
Steele suspended from the Governorship of Drury Lane (restored 1721).
Little Theatre in the Haymarket opened.
Steele's *The Theatre* (periodical) published.
Hughes' *THE SIEGE OF DAMASCUS.*

1721
Walpole became first Minister.

1722
Steele's *THE CONSCIOUS LOVERS.*

1723
Death of Susannah Centlivre.
Death of D'Urfey.

1725

Pope's edition of Shakespeare published.

1726

Death of Jeremy Collier.

Death of Vanbrugh.
Law's *Unlawfulness of Stage Entertainments* published.
Swift's *Gulliver's Travels* published.

1727

Death of George I; accession of George II.
Death of Sir Isaac Newton.
Arthur Murphy born.

1728

Pope's *The Dunciad* (first version) published.
Cibber's *THE PROVOKED HUSBAND* (expansion of Vanbrugh's fragment *A JOURNEY TO LONDON*).
Gay's *THE BEGGAR'S OPERA*.

1729

Goodman's Fields Theatre ópened.
Death of Congreve.
Death of Steele.
Edmund Burke born.

1730

Cibber made Poet Laureate.
Oliver Goldsmith born.
Thomson's *The Seasons* published.
Fielding's *THE AUTHOR'S FARCE*.
Fielding's *TOM THUMB* (revised as *THE TRAGEDY OF TRAGEDIES*, 1731).

1731

Death of Defoe.
Fielding's *THE GRUB-STREET OPERA*.
Lillo's *THE LONDON MERCHANT*.

1732

Covent Garden Theatre opened.

Death of Gay.

George Colman the elder born.

Fielding's *THE COVENT GAR-DEN TRAGEDY*.

Fielding's *THE MODERN HUS-BAND*.

Charles Johnson's *CAELIA*.

1733

Pope's *An Essay on Man* (Epistles I–III) published (Epistle IV, 1734).

1734

Death of Dennis.

The Prompter began publication (1734–1736).

Theobald's edition of Shakespeare published.

Fielding's *DON QUIXOTE IN ENGLAND*.

1736

Fielding led the "Great Mogul's Company of Comedians" at the Little Theatre in the Haymarket (1736–1737).

Fielding's *PASQUIN*.

Lillo's *FATAL CURIOSITY*.

1737

The Stage Licensing Act.

Dodsley's *THE KING AND THE MILLER OF MANSFIELD*.

Fielding's *THE HISTORICAL REGISTER FOR 1736*.